Greece & Rome

NEW SURVEYS IN THE CLASSICS No. 48

XENOPHON

BY
CAROL ATACK

Published for the Classical Association
CAMBRIDGE UNIVERSITY PRESS
2024

CAMBRIDGE UNIVERSITY PRESS
Shaftesbury Road, Cambridge CB2 8EA, United Kingdom
One Liberty Plaza, 20th Floor, New York, NY 10006, USA
477 Williamstown Road, Port Melbourne, VIC 3207, Australia
314–321, 3rd Floor, Plot 3, Splendor Forum, Jasola District Centre, New Delhi – 110025, India
103 Penang Road, #05–06/07, Visioncrest Commercial, Singapore 238467

www.cambridge.org
Information on this title: www.cambridge.org/9781009536981

Printed in Great Britain by Henry Ling Limited, The Dorset Press, Dorchester, DT1 1HD

A catalogue record for this publication is available from the British Library

ISBN 9781009536981

CONTENTS

ABBREVIATIONS

Abbreviations follow those in the *Oxford Classical Dictionary*, with some variations noted below.

DL   Diogenes Laertius, *Lives of the Philosophers*
DS   Diodorus Siculus, *Library of History*
IG   *Inscriptiones Graecae*
RO   P. J. Rhodes and R. Osborne. 2003. *Greek Historical Inscriptions. 404–323 BC.* Oxford, Oxford University Press.
SSR   G. Giannantoni. 1990. *Socratis et Socraticorum reliquiae.* Elenchos 18. Naples, Bibliopolis.

Xenophon

Ages.	*Agesilaus*
An.	*Anabasis* (*The March Upcountry*)
Apol.	*Apology* (*Defence of Socrates*)
Cyn.	*Cynegeticus* (*The Expert Hunter*)
Cyr.	*Cyropaedia* (*Education of Cyrus*)
Hell.	*Hellenica* (*History of Greece*)
Hipp.	*Hipparchicus/De equitum magistro* (*The Cavalry Commander*)
LP	*Lacedaimonion politeia* (*Constitution of the Spartans*)
Mem.	*Memorabilia* (*Memories of Socrates*)
Oec.	*Oeconomicus* (*The Estate-Manager*)
Poroi	*Poroi/De vectigalibus* (*Ways and Means*)
Symp.	*Symposium*

MAPS

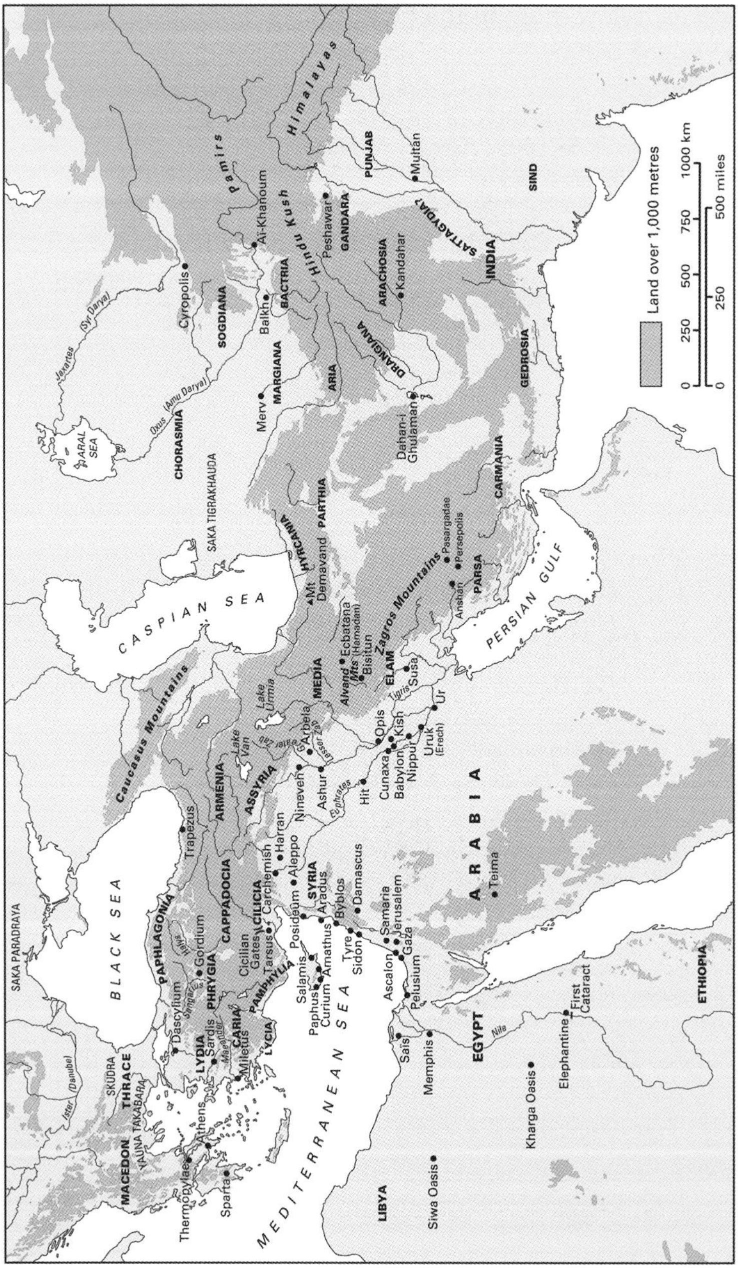

Map 1 The Achaemenid Empire

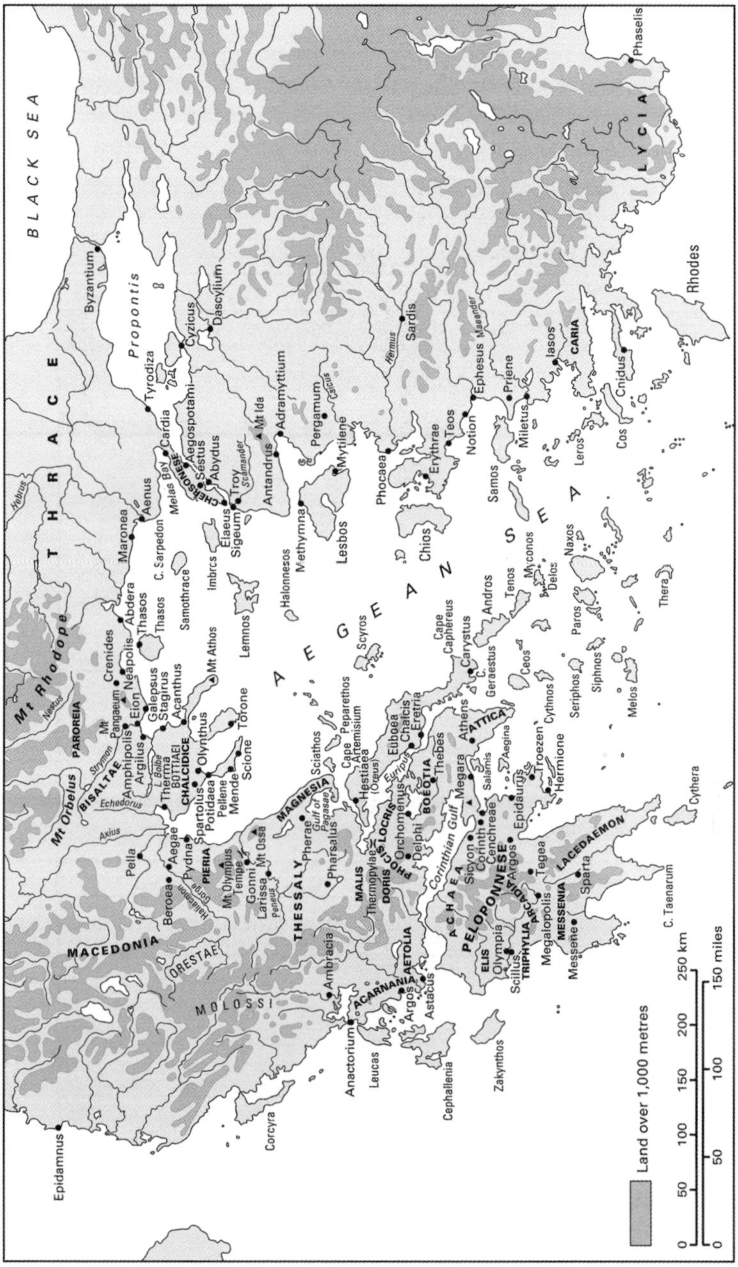

Map 2 Greece and western Asia Minor

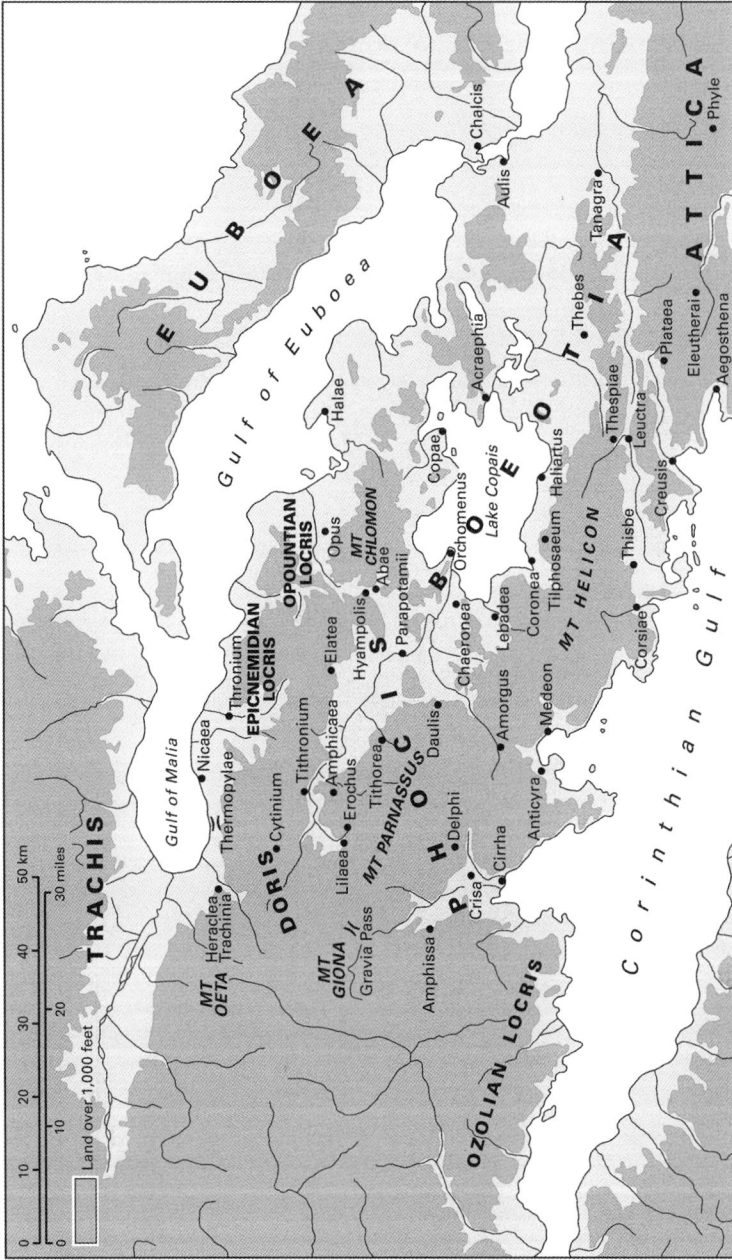

Map 3 Central Greece

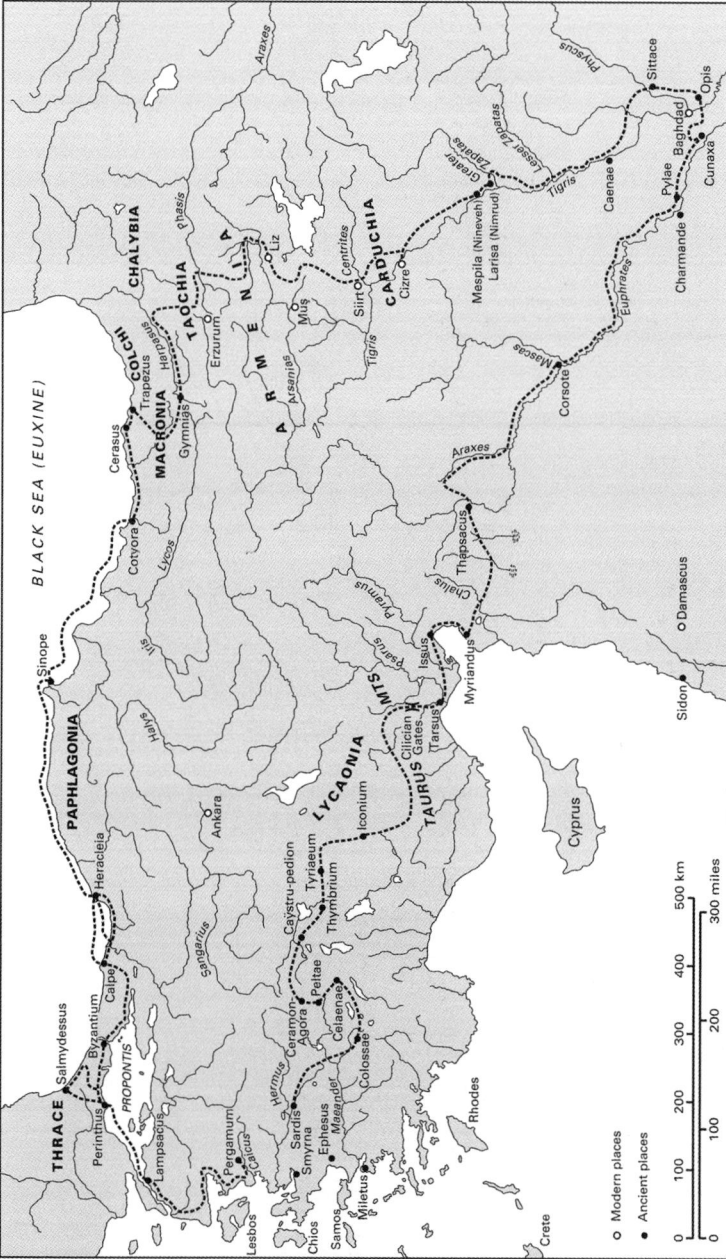

Map 4 The March of the Ten Thousand, 401–399 BC. The maps are reproduced with permission from *The Cambridge Companion to Xenophon* (ed. M. A. Flower, 2017).

I. INTRODUCTION

On the fifth day they did in fact reach the mountain; its name was Theches. Now as soon as the vanguard got to the top of the mountain, a great shout went up. [22] And when Xenophon and the rearguard heard it, they imagined that other enemies were attacking in front; for enemies were following behind them from the district that was in flames, and the rearguard had killed some of them and captured others by setting an ambush, and had also taken about twenty wicker shields covered with raw, shaggy ox-hides. [23] But as the shout kept getting louder and nearer, as the successive ranks that came up all began to run at full speed toward the ranks ahead that were one after another joining in the shout, and as the shout kept growing far louder as the number of men grew steadily greater, it became quite clear to Xenophon that here was something of unusual importance; [24] so he mounted a horse, took with him Lycius and the cavalry, and pushed ahead to lend aid; and in a moment they heard the soldiers shouting, 'The Sea! The Sea!' and passing the word along.   (*An.* 4.7.21–4)[1]

Xenophon's slow recognition that the commotion among the Greek soldiers in front of him is caused by their first glimpse of the Black Sea and the realization that they might complete their journey home, after becoming stranded in the middle of a hostile Persian empire, builds up to the cry *Thalatta! Thalatta!* It has echoed through the centuries, inspiring readers, including even those who encountered it as an adapted translation passage in Wilding's *Greek for Beginners*, the standard introduction to Greek language used in English schools in the later twentieth century.[2] Xenophon's deceptively simple narrative style has lent itself well to classroom use, but, while those who encountered him as one of the first Greek authors they read have sometimes underestimated the subtleties of his style and analysis, more recent scholarship has shown the sophistication of both.

The next chapter of this survey sets out why Xenophon is an important figure, central to our understanding of the political, social, and intellectual history of classical Athens and of interactions between Greeks and the world beyond it. It traces what we know of his life and sets it in historical context, before considering how and when he came to write his works, and what is special and distinctive about them, and showing how his works transcend boundaries of genre.

---

[1] Translation adapted from Brownson 1922.
[2] Wilding 1957: 57; Rood 2004b.

The remaining chapters treat Xenophon's thought and writing as a systematic whole, moving from the small scale of the household to the large scale of military campaign and empire. This structure reflects the importance of spatiality in his thought.[3] Xenophon's Socrates argued that leadership was the same skill applied to different domains (*Mem.* 3.4.6), and this book is organized along that principle. Starting with Xenophon's thought on life within the household and how it should be organized (Chapter III), subsequent chapters look at the relationship between citizen and city and its expression as a *politeia* (Chapter IV), Xenophon's thought on the military life, the acquisition of military skills, and their deployment on campaign (Chapter V), and his views on leadership and imperial power, the art of ruling larger entities (Chapter VI). The Conclusion moves through time as well as space, taking a necessarily selective look at Xenophon's legacy from antiquity to the present.

I would like to thank the editors of this series, John Taylor and Phil Horky, for their encouragement and patience. The anonymous reviewers provided helpful direction. Thanks to the editors, Malcolm Schofield, Tim Rood, and Emily Baragwanath for comments on earlier drafts. This book draws on my research presented at several seminars, workshops, and conferences; thanks to the organizers and participants, especially Melina Tamiolaki, Emily Baragwanath, Olga Rosius, Christopher Tuplin, and many other members of the international Xenophon community. Thanks also to the Center for Hellenic Studies, where a fellowship enabled me to begin this work, and to Newnham College, for supporting my attendance at many conferences.

I have taken some translations from Martin Hammond's *Memories of Socrates* (Hammond and Atack 2023) and from the Loeb editions. Other translations are my own, though often referring to the Loeb editions as a starting point.

---

[3] Rood 2012b.

II. XENOPHON'S THOUGHT AND STYLE

This chapter places Xenophon's systematic and comprehensive thought about the ordering of self and society in the context of his lived experience. Xenophon lived through the turbulent reordering of the Greek world as its greatest city, Athens, adjusted to its defeat in the Peloponnesian War and to the continuing contest for hegemony. In the past, he has been criticized for failings in his method, for falling short of modern disciplinary norms of historiography and philosophy. But where the scientific turn of historiography in the nineteenth century and the analytic turn of philosophy in the twentieth century caused scholars to treat Xenophon as a lesser author and thinker than Thucydides and Plato respectively, more recent scholarly developments, from the close readings of Straussians to the deployment of literary theoretical approaches such as historicism and narratology, have led to a better understanding of his distinctive achievement. The second section of this chapter uses new critical approaches to examine key features of Xenophon's prose style, ranging from its display in narrative set-piece scenes to his artful deployment of elevated rhetorical registers of language and dramatic irony. It explores his use of exemplarity to inform and educate the elite, the *kaloi kagathoi*, 'gentlemen of quality', who appear to have been his primary intended audience.[1]

An extraordinary life

Although little is known for certain about Xenophon's life, it was shaped by the circumstances of Athenian history and by the consequences of the Peloponnesian War, already underway at his birth sometime between 430 and 425 BCE – the exact date is unknown.[2] Xenophon himself gives little biographical information beyond the events he relates; other surviving ancient sources provide little more. The most detailed of these, the brief biography in Diogenes Laertius'

---

[1] Gray 2011b: 5–7; on *kaloi kagathoi*, see Hammond and Atack 2023: xxxii–xxxv.
[2] Vivienne Gray (1998: 5 n. 25) suggests the start of this range, Debra Nails (Nails 2002: 301) the end, making Xenophon two or three years younger than Plato, mostly likely born between 427 and 425.

third-century CE *Lives of the Philosophers* (DL 2.48–59), elaborates information gathered from Xenophon's own works, especially the *Anabasis*, along with other anecdotes of uncertain historicity from now lost biographies and critiques.[3] There is little further contemporary evidence. A fragment from the work of another Socratic, Aeschines, shows Xenophon in conversation with Aspasia, the partner of the general Pericles, about his love for his wife; Cicero's quotation of the work (*De inventione* 1.51–2) suggests a continuing interest in Xenophon in later antiquity.[4] That Aeschines' fragment depicts Xenophon and his wife discussing their marriage suggests that Xenophon's interest in the domestic and in marriage as a social institution was notable even among his contemporaries.[5] But it also positions Xenophon within the imaginary world of the Socratic dialogue, in which historical time is suspended.[6]

Xenophon's father, Gryllus, was a citizen of the Athenian deme of Erchia, coincidentally also the home deme of Xenophon's older contemporary, the rhetorician Isocrates (DL 2.48). Since Erchia, a rural deme to the east of the city, close to Mount Hymettus, was too far from Athens for easy return travel in a single day, the family would also have had a home in the city. Xenophon's childhood, coinciding with the early stages of the Peloponnesian War when Pericles gathered Athenians into the city in preparation for the anticipated Spartan invasion (Thuc. 2.14–16), would most likely have been spent in the city home. Perhaps, during occasional peaceful interludes such as that negotiated by Nicias and Pleistoanax in 421, Xenophon was able to spend time at Erchia and to enjoy the mountains and countryside nearby. His life-long passion for hunting (*Cynegeticus*, *Cyropaedia*) and interest in horsemanship (*Hipparchicus*, *De re equestri*) suggest that these were formative experiences for him.

As a youth from a well-off family, Xenophon might have been expected to complete his education in preparation for an active role in democratic civic life, through lessons with a teacher of rhetoric and other skills, such as the sophist Gorgias of Leontini, who visited and taught in Athens in the late fifth century and who had taught his

---

[3] Badian 2004: 35–42. Modern biographies of Xenophon include Luccioni 1948, Delebecque 1957, and Anderson 1974.

[4] Aeschines Socraticus *Aspasia*, fr. SSR VIa 70; Pentassuglio 2017; Johnson 2021: 254–7.

[5] See Chapter 3.

[6] Atack 2020b.

friend Proxenus of Thebes in Boeotia (*An.* 2.6.16).[7] Rhetorical skill was essential to a successful political career in the assembly and lawcourts of democratic Athens, a development criticized by Plato (*Gorgias, Protagoras*); Xenophon depicts himself showing just such rhetorical skill in his speeches to the Ten Thousand (*An.* 7.6.4).[8] There was also a growing interest in training in military skills, as the city's leadership roles began to demand greater technical expertise (Pl. *Laches*, although this may retroject later debates into a fifth-century context; Xen. *Hipp.*, *Mem.* 3.1, 3.3).[9]

Xenophon was familiar with the work and reputation of the leading sophists; he attributes the story of the 'Choice of Heracles' to the sophist Prodicus of Ceos (*Mem.* 2.1.21–34), although retelling it in his own style.[10] He depicts himself and others as followers of Socrates, an unconventional and informal educator, always ready to converse with fellow citizens and the young about ethical questions, and, in Xenophon's account, to offer more practical advice on questions of how to live the life of a good citizen in the context of an impoverished city.[11] Xenophon also presents himself as participating in the social practices of the Athenian elite, pursuing the beautiful Critobulus as a lover (*Mem.* 1.3.8–15), although this scenario does also provide the opportunity for his Socrates to give a critique of pederasty.

As Xenophon prepared for adult life, war and political turmoil dictated the opportunities open to him, as the city broke its peace treaties and reopened the war, and the military threat from Sparta and Persia revived and grew stronger. Athens' disastrous military adventure in Sicily (415–413 BCE) had destabilized the city's political balance and revitalized the war, now being fought on two fronts in the Aegean and on the mainland around Attica. It is unclear whether Xenophon served in the Athenian forces during the final stages of the war; J. K. Anderson and John Lee deduce that he may have ridden out in defence with the city's cavalry as a youth. Anderson adds the suggestion that he served as a marine, a role undertaken by some in the cavalry class as the naval conflict in the eastern Aegean, against

---

[7] Laks and Most 2016; Bonazzi 2020.

[8] Christ 2020: 166–7. On rhetoric in Athenian politics see Finley 1962; Ober 1989.

[9] On the lack of military training in Athens before the mid-fourth century, see Konijnendijk 2018.

[10] Whether the story told is close to Prodicus' version or Xenophon's own is much debated: see Sansone 2004, 2015; Gray 2006; Dorion 2008.

[11] See Chapters 3 and 4.

Persian-funded Spartan forces, became more significant.[12] Debra Nails, on the other hand, who argues for a later birthdate around 425, regards Xenophon as too young to have fought in this war.[13]

Xenophon's detailed account of the battle of Arginusae in 406 BCE and its aftermath (*Hell.* 1.6), and the subsequent prosecutions of the generals responsible for the lost fleet and sailors (*Hell.* 1.7), may reflect personal involvement in the events, or a growing involvement in the life of his city. The unjust treatment of generals by democratic regimes loomed large in his political thinking about democracy and the administration of justice.[14]

Within the city, these final stages of the Peloponnesian War were marked by shortages of food, especially as the routes for importing grain from the Black Sea region were blocked by the conflict. Athens was too large to feed its population from its own less productive land, although families like Xenophon's may still have managed to produce crops on their estates. Managing and surviving economic crisis is a recurrent theme of Xenophon's work (*Mem.* 2.6, 2.7; *Poroi* 1.1), although again this may reflect concerns current during the city's economic crises later in the fourth century.

Xenophon noted instances of Socrates' resistance to the Athenians' decisions when they failed to uphold their own procedures and laws: both the troubled democracy in 406 and under the oligarchic regime of the Thirty Tyrants in 404/3 (*Hell.* 1.7.15; *Mem.* 1.2.31–8). While it is unclear what his own stance or role was during this period, his writing suggests the perspective of someone who stayed in the city, albeit with decreasing enthusiasm.[15] He presents the more moderate oligarchs and the leaders of the democratic side as exemplary characters, presenting powerful speeches and scenes to the politicians Theramenes (*Hell.* 2.3.35–49) and Thrasybulus (*Hell.* 2.4.13–17, 40–2). The unifying speech he gives to the herald of the Eleusinian Mysteries, Cleocritus (*Hell.* 2.4.20–2; see Chapter 4) suggests his approval of the resolution of the civil war in 403. It is difficult, therefore, to see Xenophon either as a straightforwardly conservative figure or as a lifelong supporter of oligarchy over democracy. His

---

[12] Anderson 1974: 18–19, citing *Hell.* 1.6.24 as evidence for the use of cavalry; Lee 2005: 43–4.
[13] Nails 2002: 301.
[14] Christ 2020: 17–26; see also Chapter 4.
[15] Anderson 1974: 55–8; Badian 2004: 46–7; Christ 2020: 3.

primary concern is the fair treatment and reward of those exposed to personal risk in military and leadership roles (see Chapters 4 and 5).

Xenophon left Athens in 401 (DL 2.55), and was still absent when Socrates was tried and put to death in 399. His *Apology* relies on reports from another follower of Socrates, Hermogenes, an illegitimate son of the wealthy Athenian Hipponicus, and so half-brother of Callias, although this may be a fictive attribution, a typical feature of Socratic dialogue.[16]

Xenophon's eagerness to leave Athens and join his friend Proxenus in what developed into the expedition to replace Artaxerxes II on the Achaemenid throne with his brother Cyrus (the younger) (*An.* 3.1.4) suggests that he may have seen little personal opportunity under the restored democracy. Or, as John Lee suggests, he may, like other Athenians, have been tempted into mercenary service through financial necessity.[17] Xenophon insists that supporting this dynastic project was not the original intention of the Greeks (*An.* 3.1.9–10), but he was swept up into the mercenary campaign. The repercussions would be life-changing; Socrates' advice, warning Xenophon against being seen to support Cyrus, an ally of the Spartans, turned out to be politically acute (*An.* 3.1.5–9).

After the battle of Cunaxa, in which Cyrus was killed (*An.* 1.8.25–9.1), the 'Ten Thousand' faced many challenges, including the assassination of their original leaders. Xenophon depicted himself reluctantly taking a leading role in reorganizing the surviving members of the force, always engaging as part of a team (*An.* 3.2.32–9; see Chapter 5). He played a significant part in shepherding the Greek forces through hostile territory back to the Greek world, usually protecting the rear of the column as they travelled, and so he first experienced the famous sighting of the Black Sea as a worrying disturbance rather than a sign of safety (*An.* 4.7.21–4; see Chapter 1). However, once the Ten Thousand had reached the safety of Greek cities on the coast, rather than return to Greece, they chose to enlist on further campaigns, first with the Thracian king Seuthes (*An.* 7.3) and then, after hostility between the Thracians and Greeks grew, with Spartan forces led by Thibron attacking the Persian satrap

[16] Hermogenes, half-brother of Callias, appears as a member of the Socratic circle in Xenophon *Mem.* and *Symp.*, and Plato (*Phaedo*, *Cratylus*). Xenophon also attributes his *Hellenica* to the otherwise unknown Themistogenes of Syracuse (*Hell.* 3.1.2).
[17] Lee 2005: 42–3.

Tissaphernes (*An.* 7.6.1–7, 7.7.24). Xenophon had intended to return to Athens, a possibility which was still then open (7.7.57). However, as his account of the campaign of the Spartan king Agesilaus in Asia Minor in 396–395 shows (*Hell.* 3.4.1–4.3.4), he stayed and served with the Spartans both there and later in mainland Greece. He developed and retained a high opinion of Agesilaus as king and leader, reflected in his encomium-cum-obituary *Agesilaus*.[18] Xenophon's time in the Persian empire and on its fringes is also reflected in the descriptions of Persian life and imperial governance in his *Cyropaedia*, an extended exemplary account of the rise to power of Cyrus the Great, whose conquests in the sixth century BCE were the basis for the Achaemenid empire.[19]

After returning to Greece with Agesilaus and very likely fighting with the Spartans against his native Athens at Coronea in 395 (*Ages.* 2.6–16; see Chapter 5), there was no longer any possibility of a return to his home city, from which Xenophon appears to have been formally exiled around this time (DL 2.59). Instead, he settled in the Peloponnese at Scillous, near Olympia (*An.* 5.3.7–13), on an estate provided by the Spartans but formally in the territory of Elis. Here he lived a peaceful family life effectively outside the *polis* system, a precarious situation that his Socrates warns Aristippus about (*Mem.* 2.1.11–15).[20] He is reputed to have sent his sons, Gryllus and Diodorus, to be educated in the Spartan system of state education (DL 2.54), the much-mythologized *agōgē*.[21] Xenophon's long engagement with Sparta and its people, on campaign and within Sparta itself, makes his works a significant source for the city, although his precise stance towards Sparta as opposed to Agesilaus remains controversial.[22]

Both while on campaign and at home in peace, religious observation was an important part of Xenophon's life. He had taken to heart Socrates' criticism that he had failed to consult the Delphic Oracle correctly when planning to join Proxenus and Cyrus (*An.* 3.1.5–8). Important decisions were guided by divine omen, often revealed through sacrifice. He pictured himself celebrating a sacrifice with the community at Scillous, where he had established a shrine to the goddess Artemis (*An.* 5.3.7–8), and contributed to communal feasts.

---

[18] On Agesilaus' career, see Cartledge 1987.
[19] On Cyrus, see Briant 2002; Mitchell 2023.
[20] It is unclear whether Xenophon's wife, named Philesia (DL 2.52), was an Athenian (Badian 2004: 42).
[21] On Spartan education, see Ducat 2006.
[22] Humble 2022.

However, this was a period of disruption and change in the Peloponnese and wider Greek world, as Spartan fortunes waned and other cities rose to prominence. After Elis increasingly asserted its independence from Spartan control, Scillous was no longer a safe refuge from the constant war between Greek cities. Socrates was right again: life as a non-citizen was precarious. Xenophon and his sons moved to Corinth around 371, after the Spartan defeat at Leuctra (DL 2.56).

Both of Xenophon's sons fought as members of the Athenian cavalry, supporting Sparta against the increasingly powerful Thebes, in the battle of Mantinea in 362, but Gryllus was killed in a skirmish preceding the main battle, in which the Theban general Epaminondas died, ending Thebes's period of dominance (DL 2.54, *Hell.* 7.5.24–5). Xenophon ends his *Hellenica* at this moment of enhanced inter-*polis* upheaval but of greater personal consequence to him than to the warring cities: 'Let events to this point be the part written by me; perhaps what follows will be the concern of another' (*Hell.* 7.5.27).

Diogenes Laertius reports a story about Xenophon's response to his loss:

They say that Xenophon was at that moment performing a sacrifice, wearing a wreath, but, when his son's death was announced to him, he it took off. However, after he learned that his son had died nobly, he put the wreath back on. Some say that he did not shed a tear, but said 'I knew that I had fathered a mortal'.

(DL 2.54–5)

This anecdote, while unlikely to be historical, represents two key aspects of Xenophon's ethics: the incorporation of religious practice and piety into daily life, and the high value he placed on the courageous performance of civic and military duty.

Xenophon shows detailed awareness of Athens' financial crisis after its defeat in the Social War of 357–355, in what appears to be his final work (*Poroi*). Whether he died in Corinth, as Diogenes Laertius states (DL 2.56), or elsewhere, his attention was focused on his home city in his final years.[23] Matthew Christ argues, against William Higgins, that Xenophon's continuing concern for his native city does not presuppose his return there.[24] Perhaps Athens remained for him a city of the imagination.

---

[23] Whitehead 2019: 7–8.
[24] Higgins 1977: 128–33; Christ 2020: 3–4, see also Anderson 1974: 193.

Xenophon's life outside the *polis* structure gave him leisure to write, but there is little agreement about when his works were produced or circulated, whether they were the product of continuous effort or whether he broke off from and returned to literary activity. A historicist reading, taking account of the way in which he responds to and engages with his contemporaries, not just Plato but other Socratics, as well as writers in other historical and rhetorical genres, points to a period of intense composition later in his life, after his departure from Scillous, at a time when the legacy of Socrates was contested; this 'unitarian' view was first articulated by Schwartz and developed by Higgins.[25] Xenophon's dialogues provide exceptional evidence for the early Socratics.[26]

Scholars have taken the apparent break in the *Hellenica* – between its account of the Thirty in Athens and that of Agesilaus' campaigns against the Persians – as evidence for Xenophon's beginning writing soon after his return from active military service with Agesilaus.[27] Arguing for an early composition date for the first section of the *Hellenica*, Barthold Georg Niebuhr pointed to the apparent closure provided by the 403 oath of reconciliation (*Hell.* 2.4.43), and to Xenophon's use of the key phrase 'still to this day' (*eti kai nun*), less appropriate in the 350s than in the 390s.[28]

One pointer to later composition is the presence of anachronistic references to topics and places of fourth-century concern in dialogues apparently set in the fifth century, before the death of Socrates.[29] The discussion of conflict on the borders of Attica and Boeotia between Socrates and the younger Pericles is one example (*Mem.* 3.5.25–6). This appears linked to Athens' conflicts of the 370s and 360s, a period also documented in the *Hellenica*, rather than those of the 410s, the apparent dramatic date, given that this Pericles is presented as a youth prior to his achieving election as a general. The impossible dramatic date of the *Symposium*, and its clear response to Plato's *Symposium* in its final two chapters, also suggests later composition.[30] Some have argued that Xenophon's original work predates Plato's,

---

[25] Schwartz 1889; Higgins 1977: 99–102.
[26] Tsouna-McKirahan 1994; Vander Waerdt 1994.
[27] Dillery 1995: 24.
[28] Niebuhr 1827; and see below, n. 52.
[29] Athenaeus found multiple anachronisms in the *Symposium* (*Deipnosophistae* 5.216d–217a).
[30] Danzig 2005: 331; Gilhuly 2024, citing the detailed analysis in Thesleff 1978. See also Huss 1999a; Wohl 2004.

but this seems unlikely, as Xenophon condenses Plato's discussions, rather than Plato expanding Xenophon's.

An extraordinary body of work

Xenophon's corpus has survived complete from antiquity, although some of the shorter works and parts of longer ones may be later interpolations. Categorizing his works by genre is difficult, and is one of the reasons why this book is not arranged by work or genre; as Tim Rood has written, Xenophon is 'a strikingly innovative writer – one of the great generic experimenters of antiquity'.[31] His *Cyropaedia*, for example, contains elements of multiple established genres – Socratic dialogue, protreptic, myth, *politeia*, and more – within an overall structure, similarly to Plato's *Republic*, a work which Xenophon clearly knew.

Establishing Xenophon's intended and actual readership is also difficult. His exploration of similar themes to those of other Socratic writers, substantial intertexts with Platonic dialogue, and thematic overlap with Isocrates all suggest that he at least aimed to participate remotely in the intellectual life of the Athenian elite. The *Hipparchicus* and *Poroi* point to a more active and practical engagement with civic life, while the *Cyropaedia* and *Agesilaus* demonstrate his interest in the new genre of prose encomium and thinking on monarchy, both typified by the work of Isocrates.[32]

Even Xenophon's brief *Constitution of the Lacedaimonians* sits uneasily among other *politeia* texts, through its complex temporal structure and its focus on lifestyle and culture rather than political institutions. Like other stand-alone *politeiai*, it is argumentative and critical rather than descriptive, as is the pseudo-Xenophontic *Constitution of the Athenians*, misattributed to Xenophon in early modern times.[33] In his account of Sparta, Xenophon contrasts past and present throughout the work, leading to a penultimate chapter (which some have rejected as an interpolation) highly critical of the Spartan failure to live up to the ideals of the lawgiver Lycurgus (*LP* 14).[34] He also writes about the household and social institutions which produce citizens

---

[31] Rood 2005: xix.
[32] Pontier 2018; Atack 2020a: 122–50. See also Chapter 6.
[33] Bordes 1982: 165–203; Osborne 2017; Schofield 2021.
[34] Humble 2004, 2022: 52–61.

(*LP* 1–3), rather than focusing on the political institutions in which they interact, although fragments from the Spartan *politeia* attributed to Critias suggest a similar interest in Spartan social arrangements.[35]

Xenophon's three longest works, the *Hellenica*, *Anabasis*, and *Cyropaedia*, each inhabit multiple genres, from narrative military history to philosophical dialogue, and contain exemplary portraits of a wide range of figures, male and female, as they exert influence on events. But each has an overarching narrative arc, as does the *Memorabilia*.[36]

Although none of Xenophon's works are formally rhetorical, they contain significant speeches, both standalone and grouped, which indicate political and legal context and fill out character portraits.[37] A good example is the arrangement of grouped speeches in the *Anabasis*, at the key turning point as the Ten Thousand assess their situation and, under Xenophon's guidance, prepare to find their way home. He presents successively longer speeches addressed to successively larger groups, starting with questions addressed to himself after a prophetic dream (*An.* 3.1.13–14), and speeches to the commanders of his own group (3.1.15–25). He then addresses first the commanders of the other groups (3.1.35–44) and finally the entire force (3.2.8–32), an occasion for which Xenophon dresses up in his best armour (3.2.7), and which is interrupted by someone sneezing in the crowd (3.2.9), seized upon as an omen.[38]

Punctuating the narrative of military action with speech and debate is a structure familiar from both Homeric epic and the historiography of Herodotus and Thucydides. Other epic features that Xenophon borrows include arming scenes (such as that of Abradatas, *Cyr.* 6.4.2–9), while historiographical echoes include the rewriting of the encounter between Cyrus and Croesus originally presented by Herodotus (*Cyr.* 7.3).[39]

Originality and method in history

Xenophon's approach to the writing of history reflects the trends of his time. His central organizing method is exemplarity, with his chosen case studies inviting reflection on specific topics of leadership and

---

[35] Critias DK 88 B32 = Clem. *Str.* 6.9. See Humble 2022: 93–9.
[36] See e.g. Erbse 1961; Due 1989; Tuplin 1993; Gray 1998.
[37] Christ 2020: 156–60.
[38] Atack 2022; Rood 2004a.
[39] Gray 2011b: 119–78; Ellis 2016.

behaviour worth imitating. He deploys exemplarity both in short works such as the *Agesilaus*, built around a single exemplar, and in longer ones such as the *Cyropaedia*, which goes beyond the central exemplar of Cyrus through its many subsidiary character portraits. Even brief sketches can illuminate significant points about leadership.[40] Xenophon's assessments of character, and his crafting of valuable examples, are fully developed, and, as Frances Pownall has shown, offer 'lessons from the past for the moral instruction of his fellow aristocrats'.[41] These lessons typically present lived examples of some of the problems and examples explored more theoretically in the *Memorabilia*, another work once seen as disorganized and episodic, but whose overarching structure and argument have been recognized once again.[42] John Marincola notes that Xenophon evaluates his examples more explicitly than his predecessors had done.[43]

In the nineteenth century, proponents of the new academic discipline of historiography, such as the Danish-German scholar Barthold Niebuhr, criticized Xenophon's work for falling short of modern standards of completeness and accuracy, and for exhibiting bias rather than objectivity.[44] More recent scholars of historiography, however, have rejected the idea that 'scientific' historiography, if possible at all, is the only allowable method, and have recognized both Xenophon's clear and consistent method, and his use of exemplarity to produce a 'moral history', a model that later Greek historians such as Polybius and indeed Diodorus Siculus followed.[45]

The *Hellenica* begins as a near-continuation of Thucydides' *History of the Peloponnesian War*, and echoes Thucydidean features such as the use of speeches to convey analysis.[46] Hans-Joachim Gehrke notes that the *Hellenica* covers events during Xenophon's lifetime, and as a work of contemporary history barely engages with the past.[47] The account of the decline into tyranny of the oligarchy of the Thirty (*Hell.* 2.3–4) imposes an exemplary structure on its historical narrative and portrayal of key political actors such as Critias, leader of the Thirty (see also

[40] Flower 2015; Huitink and Rood 2016.
[41] Pownall 2004: 66.
[42] Erbse 1961; Gray 1998 illuminates the structural technique of amplification, repeating themes with greater detail.
[43] Marincola 2017: xlv.
[44] Niebuhr 1827; see Tuplin 1993: 12–18.
[45] Hau 2016; Pownall 2004.
[46] Rood 2004c.
[47] Gehrke 2023: 88–9.

Mem. 1.2.31–8).[48] Its later sections loosely track another conflict; they cover Sparta's further rise to hegemony across the Greek world and the beginning of its fall, amid the shifting balance of power among Greek cities and Athens' changing status within that balance (*Hell.* 3–8).[49] Xenophon recounts both campaigns that he experienced personally and events that show a new trend: the rise of strong military leaders such as Jason of Pherae (*Hell.* 6.1) and Epaminondas of Thebes (*Hell.* 7.4.40, 5.4–25), who threatened the dominance of Athens and Sparta. The late introduction of Epaminondas to the narrative points to Xenophon's notorious selectivity.

Xenophon does, indeed, omit significant events, such as the foundation of the Second Athenian League in 378.[50] As George Cawkwell noted, the *Hellenica* is a 'personal' account; Xenophon writes most thoroughly about people he knew, and events in which he participated, such as Agesilaus' campaign in Asia Minor (*Hell.* 3.3–4.2) and later on the Greek mainland (*Hell.* 4.3–5.4).[51] His chronology is often at odds with that of other sources, even in his relatively detailed account of the Thirty at Athens.[52]

Lisa Hau identifies various strategies by which Xenophon sets out a moral message: explicit statements, juxtapositions, and the narration of exemplars, sometimes mixing them together.[53] Some exemplary narratives are extended – the entire campaign of Agesilaus, for example, might be seen as such – while others are short and focused, such as his assessment of Teleutias, the half-brother of Agesilaus and the Spartan naval commander who sets off home garlanded by his men after defeating the Athenians off the coast of Aegina (*Hell.* 5.1.2–4). Xenophon wraps up this exemplar with an explicit evaluation:

I know that in this case I am not relating anything noteworthy in the way of expenditure or danger or planning, but, by Zeus, I think it worth a man considering what actions made his subordinates feel this way about Teleutias. For this is an action of the greatest value (*axiologōtaton*), much more than those involving great expenditure or danger.

(*Hell.* 5.1.4)

---

[48] Pownall 2019.
[49] Tuplin 1993.
[50] DS 15.28–9; *IG* II² 43. See Cawkwell 1973; Rood 2004c.
[51] Cawkwell 1979: 22–3.
[52] Krentz 1982: 131–52, tabulating Xenophon's account against that of the Aristotelian *Ath. Pol.* (25.1–38.1) and DS 14.4–33.
[53] Hau 2016: 219–20.

Note the superlative: for Xenophon, few achievements outrank successful leadership in the field. Juxtaposition, on the other hand, is a way of making implicit comment through the selection and ordering of material. As deployed by Xenophon, it is both a form of irony and a nod to Thucydides.[54] Examples are the comparison of Agesilaus with the Persian satrap Tissaphernes (*Hell.* 3.4.6, 11) and the Spartan general Lysander (*Hell.* 3.4.7–10; see Chapter 5).

The *Anabasis* contains a single overarching narrative: the story of Xenophon's adventure with the mercenaries of Cyrus, the Ten Thousand, and the return of the group after the death of Cyrus at the battle of Cunaxa in 401 (see Chapter 5). Like the *Hellenica*, it includes exemplary portraits of military and political leaders, which in this work often appear as obituaries, for Cyrus (*An.* 1.9) and the murdered generals Clearchus, Proxenus, and Meno (*An.* 2.6). As noted above, Xenophon's role is established through his speeches, but the journey home is characterized by strife among the Ten Thousand as well as the external dangers they face.

Although his focus in most works is on recent events, Xenophon's writings often feature complex temporal structures, shifting through multiple timeframes to incorporate a deeper past. Typically, his analysis slowly reveals a system which has changed for the worse. The *Lacedaimonion politeia*, for example, starts with the idea that the Spartans preserve the institutions and practices legislated by Lycurgus, which made them great. But eventually (*LP* 14) they are shown to have fallen away from the practices of which Xenophon approves.[55] A similar revelation occurs at greater scale in the *Cyropaedia*, where the final chapter (*Cyr.* 8.8) sets out how, in the present day, long-standing institutions set up by Cyrus the Great have been abandoned. Earlier in the work, their continuance into the present was indicated through the frequent use of phrases such as *eti kai nun*, 'still to this day', the phrase to which Niebuhr objected.[56]

Order and character in Xenophon's ethical system

The works most in conformity with a generic model are Xenophon's Socratic and other dialogues. While Diogenes Laertius identifies him

---

[54] For Thucydidean examples, see Rood 1998: 120–1.
[55] Humble 2022: 52–61.
[56] The phrase often appears at critical junctures and conclusions; examples include *Hell.* 2.4.43, *Mem.* 4.8.11, *Symp.* 8.2, *Cyr.* 1.2.1, 1.2.16, 7.1.45–7, 8.6.14.

as the originator of the genre (DL 2.48), many of the *Memorabilia*'s short conversations draw on and respond to Plato's dialogues, such as the discussion of friendship in Plato's *Lysis* that is echoed in Socrates' conversation with Critobulus (*Mem.* 2.6).[57] Xenophon's pointed use of characters who also appear in Plato, such as Plato's brother Glaucon (*Mem.* 3.6) and uncle Charmides (*Mem.* 3.7), as well as educators such as Hippias of Elis (*Mem.* 4.4), appears to be an act of criticism. Louis-André Dorion's major commentary on the *Memorabilia* shows the many interactions between Xenophon's work and Plato's, as well as with the thought of other Socratics such as Aristippus and Antisthenes, and the natural philosophy of Presocratic thinkers.[58] It may be helpful to see the Platonic corpus as a 'borrowed landscape' for Xenophon's philosophical writings, in which brief allusions to Plato can open a broader discussion or critique.

Xenophon explores themes and concepts in common with other Socratics, such as the master skill common to or superior to all others, labelled as the 'kingly art' (*basilikē technē*) both because it is practised by kings and because it rules over other skills (*Mem.* 2.1, 4.1; Plato *Statesman* 259d; see Chapter 6).[59] He makes specific criticism of some Socratics: Aristippus, connected with the Cyrenaics, a later hedonist school of philosophy, is Socrates' interlocutor to whom the story of the 'Choice of Heracles' between Virtue and Vice is pointedly retold (*Mem.* 2.1).[60] Like Plato, Xenophon uses historical leaders as characters to represent political and ethical positions: in a short but memorable discussion about law and justice supposedly between Pericles and Alcibiades (*Mem.* 1.2.40–6; Chapter 3); and in the *Hiero*, an imagined dialogue between the fifth-century BCE Syracusan tyrant Hiero and the epinician poet Simonides (Chapter 5).[61]

Both Xenophon's two longer Socratic dialogues, the *Symposium* and the *Oeconomicus*, explore Platonic ethical themes in Xenophontic locations.[62] The *Symposium* matches the erotic theme of Plato's version, although its setting, in a home of Callias at the Piraeus, also nods to

---

[57] Tamiolaki 2018.
[58] Dorion and Bandini 2000–11 (especially on *Mem.* 3.8–9).
[59] Dorion 2004, Atack 2020a: 98–106.
[60] Johnson 2009; Narcy 1995.
[61] Tamiolaki 2016a; see also Berkel 2020.
[62] See Chapter 2. On *Symp.*, see Christ 2020: 102–25; Johnson 2021: 187–230; Baragwanath and Verity 2022. The classic commentary on *Oec.* is Pomeroy 1994; see also Christ 2020: 72–101; Johnson 2021: 31–278; Baragwanath and Verity 2022. For a Straussian reading of both dialogues, see Pangle 2020.

Plato's *Protagoras* and *Republic*. David Johnson suggests that Xenophon's *Symposium* is intended to correct other literary accounts of Socrates' thought on *eros* and behaviour; others have argued, less plausibly, that Xenophon's work preceded Plato's.[63] The *Oeconomicus* brings together many of Xenophon's key themes, connecting the microcosm of the household to the larger scales of city, army, and empire (*Oec.* 21), and initiating a strand of social and ethical inquiry which continues with Aristotle.[64]

Xenophon's interest in spatial organization becomes a focus on good order in his philosophical works. It is identified as *taxis*, *kosmos*, or occasionally *eukosmia*, all terms which have a military origin.[65] Good order denotes both practical fitness for purpose and a broader alignment with the divine order of the cosmos; it can be instantiated at any level, from household to empire, but is of particular importance on the battlefield and on campaign, as the Athenian gentleman Ischomachus notes (*Oec.* 8.4–6).

Xenophon's ethical system is constructed consistently across his works and sets out a scheme of values, based on the Socratic pursuit of excellence (see Chapter 3), but Xenophon is more concerned than Plato with the regulation of physical appetites.[66] So for Xenophon's ideal citizen, the *kalos kagathos*, the intellectual virtue of *sōphrosunē*, a form of 'rational agency' combining self-control, moderation, and thoughtfulness, is partnered by the physical virtue of *enkrateia*, producing a combination of thoughtful behaviour and physical self-restraint.[67] Its opposite, *akrasia*, is exemplified by physical appetite uncontrolled by self-restraint, such as taking more than one's share of the delicacies at a party (*Mem.* 3.14).

Xenophon explores these virtues and their vices across a wide range of settings, from the Athenian home to cities and empires, and presents both men and women as exemplars. In this respect he is unusual among the philosophers of fourth-century Greece.[68] Virtues and vices take physical form for him; the muscular physique of an elite citizen,

---

[63] Johnson 2021: 214. See also Danzig 2005; Hobden 2005; and Huss 1999b: 415–17, with notes on parallels between *Symp.* 8.32–5 and erotic speeches in Plato's dialogues.

[64] [Arist.] *Oeconomica*; Natali 1995; Nelsestuen 2017. On the centrality of the *Oeconomicus* to Xenophon's thought, see L. Strauss 1970.

[65] Pontier 2006: 231–44.

[66] On *sōphrosunē* as a virtue, see North 1966 and Rademaker 2005.

[67] Moore 2023: 157–84. See also L. Strauss 1972; Pangle 2018; Sebell 2021.

[68] See Atack 2024; Johnson 2024; Baragwanath forthcoming.

trained in the gymnasium and exercised in the countryside, contrasts with the damaged body of the manual labourer in the city or the flabby bodies of defeated Persians exhibited by Agesilaus as a warning to Greeks of the dangers of a luxurious lifestyle (*Hell.* 3.4.19; *Ages.* 1.28), and indeed of Vice herself, with her 'abundance of flesh' (*Mem.* 2.1.22)

Xenophon expects individuals to take responsibility for maintaining and improving the skills which differentiate them from the poor and enslaved, the foreign, and women. This is particularly true of physical skills and endurance (*karteria*), which benefit from practice (*askēsis*) through activities such as hunting. Encouraging others in the development and maintenance of their skills, and ensuring that they stick to their tasks and responsibilities, are key parts of leadership as managerial oversight (*epimeleia*; see Chapter 4). The *Cyropaedia* is framed as an inquiry into the superlative leadership skills of Cyrus the Great (*Cyr.* 1.1.1–6; see Chapters 5 and 6), while much of the *Memorabilia* details Socrates' ability to impart such skills (Chapter 4). The *Anabasis* provides a series of case studies of leadership in adversity, including critical notes on Spartan leadership (Chapter 6). The ability to impart practical skills to the domestic workforce is equally evidence of leadership skill, exemplified by the wealthy Athenian Ischomachus, who trains both his wife and his (enslaved) workforce well (*Oec.* 7–10, 12–14; Chapter 3).

Xenophon is also concerned with interpersonal relations in the context of civic and military life. This is expressed through the concepts of *charis* and *philia*, both concerning personal relationships of reciprocity. *Philia* is the value invoked in the traditional Greek concern with 'helping friends and harming enemies'; Xenophon devotes much of the second book of the *Memorabilia* to exploring Socrates' thought on how friendships should be created and maintained, and how they might be valued (see Chapter 3).[69] *Charis* is the reciprocal exchange of favours, gifts, and influence, which operates between family members, between democratic citizens in the *polis*, and between powerful rulers like Cyrus and his subjects. Vincent Azoulay describes it as a 'compelling norm' which nonetheless was frequently flouted, making ingratitude a vice which Xenophon frequently criticizes in many kinds of social relationships, from parent and child to leader and citizen body.[70] While *charis* governs many relationships and exchanges, Xenophon is also, in

---

[69] Tamiolaki 2018; Berkel 2020. For the wider context, see Blundell 1991.
[70] Azoulay 2018a: 21–2.

common with other fourth-century thinkers, much concerned with the question of the just distribution of material and immaterial goods among incommensurate non-equals. The distribution of the spoils of war between those who have made different contributions to their capture offers a pressing example of this problem, addressed explicitly by Cyrus (*Cyr.* 2.2–4; Chapter 6).

At the same time, Xenophon's works were reinterpreted by the political philosopher Leo Strauss and his followers, who treated them as 'esoteric' texts with meanings concealed from non-initiates. Some scholars draw on this tradition to deny that Xenophon is an ethicist and to present him as a 'realist', seeking pragmatic solutions to political problems without concern for custom or morality, citing Xenophon's Cyrus as the key exemplar as he builds his empire and cements personal control over it.[71] Such readings explore the explicitly military and political elements of Xenophon's work, especially the *Cyropaedia* and its account of Cyrus' rise to power, and the regime transition ('republic to empire') between the limited monarchy of Persia and the autocratic empire that Cyrus creates. They observe how Cyrus is taught by his father to use deceit as a management tool (*Cyr.* 1.6; see Chapter 6), and how he employs those techniques himself to outmanoeuvre his uncle Cyaxares for command and loyalty of the Median forces (*Cyr.* 5.5; see Chapter 6).[72] Cyrus becomes not a positive exemplar for imitation, but a warning to those tempted to imitate him.[73]

Twentieth-century analytic philosophers, like nineteenth-century historians, saw little of value in Xenophon's portrait of Socrates, compared with Plato's version with his emphasis on dialectic and intellectual puzzles, and the epistemology and metaphysics of the *Republic* and *Phaedo*, topics largely (though not entirely) absent from Xenophon's Socratic works. These critics imagined the real-life Xenophon, in J. K. Anderson's words, 'hanging around the outskirts of a discussion, picking up something of the manner but not the matter'.[74] Bertrand Russell was damning in his assessment of 'a stupid man's report of what a clever man says', but, as Gregory Vlastos noted,

---

[71] Strauss's key contributions include L. Strauss 1972 (*Memorabilia*) and L. Strauss 2013 (*Hiero*); see Burns 2015. Critiques of Straussian approaches to Xenophon include Dorion 2001 (*Mem.* 4.4); Gray 2011b (focused on the *Cyropaedia*); and Rood 2015 (*Anabasis*).

[72] See Chapter 5. 'Republic to empire' readings of the *Cyropaedia* include Newell 1983 and Nadon 2001.

[73] See Reisert 2009.

[74] Anderson 1974: 21.

Xenophon is 'anything but a stupid man' who 'displays shrewd judgement', and his work presents important testimony, albeit in Vlastos' view limited in understanding of the philosophical details.[75]

More recently, scholars such as Louis-André Dorion have shown how Xenophon's dialogues contain a distinctive and coherent presentation both of a system of thought and also of the contested legacy of Socrates.[76] In this reading, the *Memorabilia* engages extensively with the work of Plato and with other Socratics such as Aristippus and Antisthenes, and provides important evidence for the early reception of the natural philosophy of Presocratic thinkers.[77]

The 'dark' readings of Straussians have been opposed by those working within the more literary and humanistic field of Classics, whose readings acknowledge the complexity and nuance of Xenophon's writing along with its literary and humanistic qualities. Literary scholars such as Vivienne Gray have rediscovered the strengths of Xenophon's work and have reasserted the seriousness of his endeavour and the skill with which he carries it out.[78] Sarah Pomeroy, Emily Baragwanath, and others have shown how his focus on the home and the personal makes a distinctive contribution at odds with the often misogynistic context of the Greek world.[79]

Style and language

From antiquity onwards, Xenophon's writing – and indeed his person – have been praised for their charm and beauty. Diogenes Laertius described Xenophon himself as 'very handsome' (DL 2.48), adding that 'he was called the Attic muse for the sweetness of his style' (DL 2.57), and that this led to Plato's rivalry with him. Another ancient literary critic, Demetrius, noted that Xenophon was able to deploy 'charm' through skilful writing (*On Style* 134, 137–9). Cicero wrote that 'the Muses were said to speak with the voice of Xenophon' (*De oratore* 62).[80] However, although Xenophon's style was much

---

[75] Vlastos 1991: 101, citing Russell 1945: 83. Vlastos praised the wit of Xenophon's *Symposium*. See Irwin 1974 for a strong statement of this critique of Xenophon.

[76] Best summarized in Dorion 2017; fully set out in Dorion and Bandini 2000–11; Dorion 2013; and Dorion and Bandini 2021.

[77] Sedley 2007: 78–86.

[78] E.g. Gray 1998, 2011b.

[79] E.g. Pomeroy 1994; Baragwanath 2002.

[80] See Gray 2017 and Rood 2017b.

discussed in antiquity, it is only more recently that scholars have used modern techniques of literary and linguistic analysis to demonstrate the careful composition of his work. Narratologists, for example, have shown how artfully he constructs his narratives, and how apparent digressions emphasize important themes.[81] The flashback to Xenophon's conversation with Socrates before his departure from Athens, for example, is positioned in the *Anabasis* at the point when the character Xenophon begins to emerge as a leader deploying Socratic values (*An.* 3.1.5–7).

Xenophon offers readers a mixture of vivid narrative, dramatic tableaux, witty dialogue, and impassioned speeches. He also comments on and connects his narrative and analysis to those of other writers, such as Plato in his Socratic works, although these references are often oblique and unmarked. There may, therefore, be other allusions to Socratic texts by other authors whose texts are lost; his accounts of Socrates' encounters with Antiphon (*Mem.* 1.6) and Antisthenes, for example (*Mem.* 2.5; *Symp.* 4.34–44), hint at continuing debates, the full details of which are unknowable. Echoes of other texts and writers feature across his work; as noted above, his historical writing is in dialogue with Thucydides and his philosophical writing with Plato, and like Plato he often nods to Homer and the epic tradition.

Xenophon's descriptive tableaux are a notable feature of his narrative work, incorporating both description and implicit commentary on the scene and events, often delivered through intertextual parallels with Homeric epic and historiography.[82] His account of the return of Alcibiades to Athens from exile in 408/7 (*Hell.* 1.4.12–16) demonstrates these features, recalling Thucydides' depiction of the departure of the Sicilian expedition from Athens' port in 415 (Thuc. 6.31.1–32.2), and of the arrival of news of its defeat in 413 (Thuc. 8.1.1–2). Alcibiades, of course, had sailed with the Sicilian expedition as one of its generals, but did not return, as he went into traitorous exile in Sparta. Xenophon's account contains features of both Thucydidean passages, and follows Thucydides in focalizing the departure scene through the responses of the watching crowds:

When [Alcibiades] saw that the city was favourable to him and that he had been elected a general, and his friends had privately sent for him, he sailed into the Piraeus on the

---

[81] E.g. Rood 2012a, 2012b.
[82] Gray 2011b.

day when the city celebrates the Plynteria, and the shrine of Athena is covered up, which some people thought was prejudicial both for him and the city. For no-one in the city would dare to undertake any serious business on this day. But when he sailed in, a crowd both from Piraeus and the city, gathered by the ships, wandering about and wanting to see Alcibiades. Some were saying that he was the strongest of the citizens and he alone had been unjustly exiled, and that those less capable than him had plotted against him, making even more shameful allegations and conducting politics in their own private interest, while that man had always increased public resources both from his own and the city's capacity…but others said that he alone was responsible for their past troubles, and that the things they feared happening to the city were a risk if he alone were in place as a leader.   (Xen. *Hell*. 1.4.12–17)

Xenophon evokes both the excitement of the scene and the division of opinion about Alcibiades among the Athenians between the positive and the negative, alerting the reader to the political conflict which materializes in the subsequent narrative. His characteristic focus on religious detail – the inauspicious day of the return – here echoes the unusual prominence of religion in Thucydides' account, where the expedition's departure had been accompanied by prayers and libations (Thuc. 6.32.1–2), and its failure by anger against seers (Thuc. 8.1.1). Xenophon also sets up future steps in the narrative: Alcibiades is met on his arrival by his cousin Euryptolemus (*Hell*. 1.4.19), who will later speak in defence of the generals prosecuted after the battle of Arginusae (*Hell*. 1.7.12, 16–34).[83]

Xenophon uses similarly vivid scenes to set up important narrative strands in the *Cyropaedia*, as when the courtier Araspas describes his first encounter with the Asian queen Pantheia, who has been captured after Cyrus' forces defeated her husband's allies in a key battle. Araspas describes what he saw when he went to explain her fate to her:

when we entered her tent, we didn't identify her at first. For she was sitting on the ground with all her attendants around her. Then, since we wished to know which was the mistress, we looked around, and at once she seemed different from all the other women, even though she was sitting with her head covered and looking at the ground. When we ordered her to get up, all the women around her got up with her, and she was distinguished first by her height, then by her excellence and graceful posture, even though she was wearing humble clothing. It was clear that her tears were flowing, some down her dress, others even to her feet.   (*Cyr*. 5.1.4–6)

At this point, the oldest of Araspas' party explains to Pantheia that she is being allotted to Cyrus, and Araspas reports her reaction:

---

[83] See Chapter 4 for a detailed reading of the trial.

When the woman heard this, she tore her outer clothing from top to bottom and wailed; her attendants cried along with her. At that moment the greater part of her face became visible, and her neck and arms too. You can be sure, Cyrus, that I, and all the others who saw her, agreed that there was not a mortal woman of such a kind in Asia. But you absolutely must see her yourself.   (*Cyr.* 5.1.6–7)

This scene further exemplifies the way in which Xenophon exploits the power of looking, and of the description of spectacle, as the queen's attendants act in chorus with her; there may be some orientalism in play in his presentation of the sights of Cyrus' court and its exoticized captives.[84] As with the Ten Thousand's sighting of the sea, he reveals details gradually, as Pantheia becomes visible. Araspas' narration also exemplifies Xenophon's control of his narrative through the use of irony. In this case, Araspas will later become obsessed with Pantheia's beauty, and will stalk and harass her, threatening her with sexual assault (*Cyr.* 6.1.31–7; see Chapter 6); his initial description of her hints at this later development.

Xenophon's varied diction, which incorporates different dialectical forms and military and technical language, further enriches the texture of his prose. His careful use of Ionic and Doric dialect forms contributes to the overall effect of his writing, and indeed may better represent the Athenian language of his time than the 'pure' Attic of the orators.[85] Huitink and Rood note that this development is anticipated by the Old Oligarch (ps-Xen. *Ath. Pol.* 2.8) and also suggest that Xenophon deploys non-Attic forms to internationalize his work for a wider readership, pointing to their greater presence in works such as the *Cyropaedia* which are not focused on Athens itself.

Using technical language enabled Xenophon to make precise points about military action, as well as adding colour and interest. Huitink and Rood note that military jargon itself is often metaphorical, such as the use of parts of the body to describe a column of troops (for example *pleurai*, 'flank', at *An.* 3.2.36). They add that this use of technical terms represents a development in historiography which is continued by Polybius.[86]

---

[84] Whitmarsh 2018: 62–72 on cultural hybridity in the *Cyropaedia*; see also Chapter 6, and Harman 2008, 2023: 117–23. Xenophon's description of the *hetaira* Theodote's home (*Mem.* 3.11) receives a similar treatment: see Goldhill 1998.
[85] Huitink and Rood 2019: 27–9.
[86] Huitink and Rood 2019: 31–2.

Xenophon's use of speeches contributes to the management of narrative pace, pausing the action while its significance is made explicit. His authorial judgements echo the style of his speeches – Huitink and Rood note the presence of *pan-* compounds, denoting scale and universality.[87] He uses strings of superlatives to emphasize important points, as at *Mem.* 3.3.9, where he argues that people are especially (*malista*) obedient to the best (*beltistous*) and most knowledgeable experts in their field – from medicine (*iatrikōtaton*) to helmsmanship (*kubernētikōtaton*) and farming (*georgikōtaton*). The herald Cleocritus' reconciliatory speech to the warring Athenians uses similar language to emphasize important religious and cultural arguments (*Hell.* 2.4.21–2).

Finally, Xenophon makes consistent use of vivid imagery to illustrate his political points, including collapsing image and referent with troubling political and ontological implications. Some of this imagery is traditional and Homeric, such as the analogy between kings and shepherds (*Cyr.* 8.2.14), which characterizes rule and leadership as a form of care:[88]

Why do you think Homer called Agamemnon 'shepherd of the people'? Is it because the shepherd must see to it that his sheep are safe and have what they need, so that the purpose for which they are kept is achieved?   (*Mem.* 3.2.1)

Xenophon appears at times to take the implicit consequences of this image – that those under the care of rulers are inferior to them in the same way that animals are to their human shepherds – as evidence that social hierarchies have a natural cause in the essential nature of the parties in the relationship. The uneducated, women and young men alike, are likened to unbroken and untrained animals (*Symp.* 2.10–11; *Mem.* 4.1.3; *Oec.* 3.10–11). And, like Plato, he collapses the personal status of enslavement with the political experience of unfreedom (*Mem.* 2.1, 3.5).

Conclusion

Xenophon's unusual life influenced the topics about which he wrote, from his encounters with Socrates to his experiences of the Persian empire and its rulers. His varied works often sit uneasily within modern

---

[87] Huitink and Rood 2019: 34–6.
[88] Brock 2004; Atack 2020c.

classifications of literary genre. However, all share features such as a focus on exemplary narrative, the use of speeches to convey judgement, and a consistent and systematic ethics with a Socratic heritage, focused on values such as self-control and generosity. While philosophers and historians aligned to some methodologies have disputed the value of his work as evidence for the thought of Socrates or the history of Athens, more sophisticated evaluations by current scholars have demonstrated the skill with which Xenophon crafts his vivid narratives and analysis, across and between different genres.

III. THE GREEK HOUSEHOLD AND PERSONAL RELATIONSHIPS

Xenophon's thought on life and relationships within the household yields compelling insights into domestic life in ancient Greek cities, and attitudes towards the personal relationships which connected citizens to each other. The household also provides a location in which values and knowledge are transmitted between husband, wife, and subordinate workers (*Oeconomicus*), and in which discussions between friends and citizens can take place (*Symposium*). The presence of Socrates signals the normative and prescriptive element of these works. The good order of the household, and the behaviour of husband and wife within it, can be paralleled in Xenophon's taxonomy of social organization with the order of society at the level of city, army, and empire. The placing of the domestic within this normative structure means that one should be cautious in interpreting his work as straightforwardly descriptive of Athenian domestic life.[1]

Xenophon's focus on the home fits into a tradition of didactic 'economic' texts, beginning with the seventh-century epic Hesiod's *Works and Days*, through to the texts from later antiquity which make up the pseudo-Aristotelian *Oeconomica*. But he also, according to Sarah Pomeroy, displays a new and unusual focus on marriage as a partnership for 'production and reproduction'.[2] This emphasis on marriage is accompanied by a distinctive approach to the other personal relationships of a citizen explored in the *Memorabilia*, particularly emotional and sexual relationships with other citizen men (*Mem.* 2.6; *Symp.*) and with female sex workers (*Mem.* 3.11).

Xenophon is particularly concerned with the life and development of the *kalos kagathos*, a 'fine and good' elite citizen, exemplified by the wealthy Ischomachus, who fits an ethical and aesthetic ideal, and whose ethos and actions in managing his estate are unimpeachably correct. Most citizens fall short of that ideal; whether Socrates himself meets the criterion is debatable.[3]

---

[1] Compare the topics and organization of Aristotle's *Politics* Book 1; see Schmitt Pantel 1992: 78–9; Natali 1995.

[2] Pomeroy 1994: 41–6.

[3] L. Strauss 1972, with further argument by Danzig 2003b.

The household as microcosm

The household is a microcosm of larger forms of human coexistence: the *polis*, the army, and the empire. Xenophon regards the management of all as similar exercises undertaken at different scales. His Socrates tells a soldier disappointed at being defeated in the election for a post as a commander by a man whose experience lay in estate management:

> Don't underestimate the men who manage estates (*tōn oikonomikōn andrōn*), Nicomachides. The management of a private business differs only in scale from the management of public affairs, and in other respects they are very similar, notably and most importantly in that neither can be done without the involvement of people, and there is no distinction between the people involved in private and public operations – those in charge of public affairs are dealing with just the same sort of people as private managers.
> (*Mem.* 3.4.12)[4]

The idea that there was a single art of leadership or management which could be exercised at all levels, from household to empire, was a conventional view in fourth-century Greek thought, shared to some extent by Plato (*Statesman* 258e) but criticized by Aristotle, who countered that the rule of such different domains represented qualitatively different skills (*Politics* 1.1.1252a7–18).[5] Xenophon, like Plato, identifies this general supervisory skill as the 'kingly art' (*basilikē technē*), but he claims that it applies to the household as much as the kingdom; the rule of a despotic king is effectively conducted over a very large household.

The household, like the cosmos itself, benefits from good order, something that is always of prime concern to Xenophon. Ischomachus tells his wife: 'there is nothing so useful (*euchrēston*) or so good (*kalon*) for human beings as order (*taxis*)' (*Oec.* 8.3).[6] The satisfaction is both aesthetic and practical, inside the home and beyond it, from the holds of trading ships (*Oec.* 8.11–16) to military formations for battle and display, and the arrangements of choruses of performers. A 'well-ordered' (*kata kosmon*) house can be a 'chorus of equipment' (*Oec.* 8.20).

In writing about the household, Xenophon usually focuses on its legal head, the male citizen, who in other contexts might be the ruler

---

[4] Trans. Hammond in Hammond and Atack 2023.
[5] Brock 2004: 247–9; Atack 2020a: 152–62.
[6] Higgins 1977: 28–9; Pontier 2006: 238.

of a city or empire or the leader of an army. All are complex organizations in which tasks should be distributed to specialist staff, but the leader must synthesize and oversee the whole organization, provide direction, and spot opportunities, while occasionally delegating to others – which means his wife and the better trained of his enslaved workers. Home is also the centre of wider social and familial networks. In the second book of the *Memorabilia*, Xenophon covers the relationships such a man might need to manage: those between parents and children (2.2), competitive brothers (2.3), and the problems of male citizens as heads of household dealing with financial hardship (2.7) and needing to seek employment (2.8).

Xenophon shows some empathy towards the situation of citizen wives, who have equal capacity to contribute to the household (*Oec.* 7.26–8) and exercise the same forms of oversight. Less often, this extends to those few heads of household who are not male citizens, such as the *hetaira* Theodote, a non-citizen woman who depends on financial support from 'friends' paying for companionship and sexual services to fund her household (*Mem.* 3.11). And he shows some interest in the activities of the enslaved members of the household.

Xenophon's account of Spartan customs and values related to family life reads as being also a criticism of Athens. His Spartan *politeia* begins with a discussion of the home in the context of birth and early childhood (*LP* 1.3–10); but Spartan men's lives would eventually be focused on their messes, outside the household. Sparta offers a different split between the public and private aspects of life from that of Athens (*LP* 5.5–7, 6.1–5), affecting the roles of men and women.

Socrates at home

The personal lives and domestic arrangements of philosophers who promoted alternative lifestyles or questioned everyday living arrangements would become a topos of the Hellenistic and later biographical tradition, also seen in pseudepigraphic texts such as the letters supposedly from the Cynic philosopher Crates to his wife Hipparchia (DL 6.96–8; *Letters of Crates* 28–33).[7] Xenophon, in depicting Socrates at home with his family, stands at an early stage in

---

[7] Rosenmeyer 2001: 221–4.

this tradition, although other Socratics clearly treated similar topics, often using the same characters.[8]

Most surviving Socratic dialogues present the philosopher engaging with a wide range of interlocutors away from his own home, placing him in Athens' public spaces and the private homes of its elite. Plato shows Socrates' wife and children being dismissed from the scene on his final day (Pl. *Phd.* 116b). However, Xenophon depicts Socrates at home, in a dialogue with his son Lamprocles that plays a key structural role in the *Memorabilia*.[9] For Thomas Pangle, the reader is 'plunged down' in a 'roller-coaster drop' from the lofty discussion of Heracles' choice in the previous chapter, but this changed setting asserts the importance of the family for Xenophon.[10] After the *Memorabilia*'s first book, which offers an initial defence of Socrates against the actual twin charges of impiety (*Mem.* 1.1) and corrupting the youth (*Mem.* 1.2) levelled against him in 399 BCE, Xenophon turns to depicting his teacher as a source of wise advice to family and friends, beginning in his own home, as further evidence against the charges. The relationship between parents and sons was fundamental to Athenian piety; families were also responsible for choosing their sons' educators.[11] Respect for parents was an aspect of character scrutinized as part of the *dokimasia*, preliminary due diligence hearings held for appointees to political office.[12]

Xenophon turns the focus from the father–son relationship to that of mother and son. Lamprocles has been complaining to Socrates about his mother's critical attitude to him, but the latter tells him to stop being ungrateful and to listen to her (*Mem.* 2.2.1–2), placing the question of gratitude to parents within a wider context of civic justice.[13] He describes the contribution that both parents make to their children's lives, highlighting the personal risk borne by the mother:

Once she has conceived, the woman carries this burden, growing heavy with the weight of it, risking her life, and nourishing it with its share of her own food. And then after all she has suffered in carrying it to term and giving birth, she feeds and cares for it, even though the baby has done her no favour so far and has no notion of who is looking after

---

[8] See Aeschines *SSR* VIA 70 = Cic. *Inv. rhet.* 1.51–3; Johnson 2021: 254–5.
[9] Erbse 1961; Gray 1998: 130–2.
[10] Pangle 2018: 80.
[11] B. Strauss 1993: 19.
[12] [Arist.] *Ath. Pol.* 45.3, 55.2–4; Lysias' *dokimasia* speeches (Lys. 16, 25, 26, 31) give a flavour of the kinds of argument used.
[13] Pangle 2018: 84.

it so well. It cannot even indicate what it wants, but the mother has to guess at its needs and likes and try to supply them: and she continues to feed it for a long time, putting up with that labour by day and night, and not knowing what thanks she will get for her efforts.   (*Mem.* 2.2.5)[14]

The relationship between mother and infant is marked by its lack of reciprocity: infants can offer no immediate reward for the labour expended on them, and may not survive into adulthood. Xenophon shows that, unlike other civic relationships, mothers must give care without expecting any return. The sculpted gravestones of Athenian women who died in childbirth are testimony to both the risks of the relationship and its importance.[15]

Xenophon plays with and subverts more conventional negative views of women in the *Symposium*. Unlike Plato, he presents the symposium as a space in which women performers are welcome participants, although, unlike the male guests, the female entertainers do not speak. Socrates points to the skills of the girl dancer who has performed juggling tricks for the diners, and observes that she demonstrates the capacity of women to learn:

'In many other actions, and in the actions the girl is performing, it's clear that the nature of women is really no worse than that of a man, but she lacks strength and understanding (*gnōmē*). And so if any of you has a wife, let him teach her whatever he would like her to know and use.'

And Antisthenes said, 'How, Socrates, do you know this and yet not educate Xanthippe, and use a woman who is in my opinion the most difficult of all who ever were or shall be?'   (*Symp.* 2.9–10)

Socrates responds with an analogy to training horses; his experience with his difficult wife will make him better at educating any other woman. The analogy between dominating women and breaking a horse, seeing the young girl as the untamed colt, was familiar from poetry (for example, Soph. *Ant.* 477–8), but fits neatly into Xenophon's wider use of human–animal interactions to describe social hierarchies.[16]

---

[14] Trans. Hammond in Hammond and Atack 2023.

[15] For example, a funerary stele showing a seated woman as her (slave) attendant takes the baby away, British Museum 1894,0616.1.

[16] Sophocles uses the image for both political and social domination; see Griffith 2000 ad 477–8. Xenophon also uses the analogy to describe the uneducated (*Mem.* 4.1.3).

Women's lives at home

Although Xenophon's depictions of women of free citizen status reinforce a particular view of the division of labour between the sexes, he nonetheless accords such women agency in the management of their homes and the stewardship of family resources and property, and credits them with skill and knowledge for doing so. While women are often presented as consumers of resources (Hesiod, *Works and Days* 702–5; Semonides fr. 7) and disruptive to the order and continuity of families – notably in Athenian tragedy, where Sophocles' Antigone and Euripides' Medea are only two examples of women who prevent the orderly continuation of the family – Xenophon shows women as co-workers in a joint enterprise, to which each partner contributes different but valuable skills and labour.[17] He incorporates women, still treated as opposite to and at times dependent on men in a binary divide, within a positive and orderly microcosm of the larger cosmos.

In his *Oeconomicus*, Xenophon shows Socrates advising Critobulus, the son of his friend Crito, on household management and marriage through an extended report of a conversation with an idealized Athenian citizen and estate-owner, Ischomachus.[18] Socrates regards the relationship between husband and wife as depending on the wife's being trained by the husband in the common goal of preserving household wealth:

'I can show you men who use their wives so that they are fellow workers in increasing their household, and those who do so in a way which causes them a very great deal of grief.'

'In this case, Socrates, is the man to blame or the woman?'

'When a flock of sheep is for the most part bad,' Socrates said, 'we blame the shepherd, and when a horse is mostly bad, we criticize the rider; but in the case of a woman, if she has been taught good actions by her husband and then does bad things, perhaps it would be right for the woman to take the blame; but if he didn't teach her good and fine action (*ta kala kagatha*) and used her while she was ignorant of these things, wouldn't it be right to blame the husband?'   (*Oec.* 3.10–11)

The situation Socrates describes reflects Athenian elite marriage practices, which were quite different from modern 'companionate'

---

[17] Cf. Pl. *Meno* 71e, possibly drawing on Gorgias.

[18] Critobulus' need for education drives the discussion in Plato's *Euthydemus*; he is also present in Xen. *Symp.*, and mentioned in Pl. *Ap.* and *Phd.* See Nails 2002: 116–19.

marriage. In a society where men of citizen status were not treated as fully independent adult citizens and did not marry till reaching the age of roughly thirty, the young women they married were chosen by their family and were typically in their mid-teens, but ready to bear children. Xenophon recasts the inequality of age, experience, and education in these marriages as a pedagogic opportunity for the husband: he can teach his wife to act in a manner appropriate to a *kalos kagathos* like himself.[19] Ischomachus' wife was 'not yet fifteen' when they married (*Oec.* 7.5), and Critobulus admits to Socrates that his wife was young and uneducated when they married (3.13), and that he does not often engage her in conversation, despite her important role in the home (3.12).[20] Xenophon, however, mentions a woman who did have a companionate relationship, Pericles' partner Aspasia, whom Socrates offers to introduce to Critobulus: 'I shall introduce you to Aspasia, who will give proof (*epideixei*) of all these things more expertly (*epistēmonesteron*) than I can' (*Oec.* 3.14).

Aspasia is an intriguing counter-example to Ischomachus' wife. As a non-citizen woman brought up in Miletus, in an aristocratic context outside Athens, she had both a different education from Athenian women and a different kind of relationship with Pericles from that experienced in a typical citizen marriage.[21] She featured in dialogues by several Socratics. Xenophon's Socrates here grants her epistemic authority, and the formal ability to demonstrate her knowledge as an *epideixis*.[22] He follows this by outlining women's key role in maintaining the household, and the space in which it is exercised:

> I think that a woman who is a good partner in the household is the counterweight to her husband. For the goods which come into the house do so for the most part through the actions of the man, while most of the expenditure comes about through the woman's stewardship. And when these things are done well, the household grows, and when they are done badly, it shrinks.   (*Oec.* 3.15)

Xenophon notes the importance of women's work in managing expenditure, but also in domestic production and preservation. Women were responsible for a range of endeavours critical to family life and the maintenance of resources: the preservation and storage of

---

[19] Cox 2010; Glazebrook and Olson 2013.
[20] Pomeroy 1994: 268–9.
[21] This unusual status also attracted ridicule from comic poets (Ar. *Ach.* 526–9; see Henry 1995: 19–28; Kennedy 2014: 74–8).
[22] Cf. Pl. *Menex.* 235e–236b.

food, the production of textiles and clothing, and the management of domestic labour. Women's work also had an economic value, even if it was realized only in certain circumstances; in poorer households, textiles and other goods might be produced for sale in the market. Socrates advises Aristarchus, who has taken in many female relatives during the civil conflict of 403, to encourage these women to produce cloaks for sale, so that the household's resources are not depleted by the costs of their subsistence (*Mem.* 2.7).

Aristarchus observes that the civil war has damaged many parts of the economy, which means that he cannot raise funds by selling his household goods (*Mem.* 2.7.2). Socrates provides examples of Athenian entrepreneurs who are succeeding in business, and the two consider whether it is proper for women of free citizen status to work in craft businesses, as enslaved workers do (2.7.6–7). Socrates' advice balances this consideration with the assumption that these women, too, would rather take responsibility and action for their upkeep than sit in idleness and worry about their diminishing resources. He concludes with a delicately phrased point that textile skills are 'the most honourable and decorous for women' (2.7.10) – perhaps a hint about sex work, a less honourable form of labour for citizen women, and one paralleled with textile work in literary and visual sources.[23] Exercising their best skills will both bring the women satisfaction and secure the economic stability of the household.

Women's work with textiles was part of an order that Xenophon regards as natural, in which tasks are organized and in turn gendered by their location within or outside the household, creating a strict binary division. Ischomachus sets out this order to the young wife whom he is 'training':

Since we know what tasks have been set in place (*prostetaktei*) for each of us by the god, my wife, we must try to perform the tasks which are appropriate to each to the best of our abilities. Indeed the law, which yoked together man and wife, joins in approval; just as the god made them partners (*koinōnous*) in their children, so the law makes them partners [in the house]. And the law ordains that those acts in which the god made each of them more capable are good. For it is finer (*kallion*) for the woman to remain indoors than to be out in the fields, and it is more shameful (*aischion*) for the man to stay indoors rather than taking care of business outdoors. And if a man acts in a way contrary to that established in nature by the god, the god does not fail to notice his

---

[23] Ar. *Lys.* 574–86; McClure 2015.

disorderly behaviour (*ataktōn*) and punishes him for neglecting his own work (*amelōn*) and for doing a woman's work.   (*Oec.* 7.29–31)

Xenophon here shows how good law mirrors and helps to protect the natural order of the cosmos, as ordained by the gods, collapsing the *nomos*/*physis* distinction used by Greek thinkers of this time.[24] The concern about taking care of and performing one's own work reflects a core principle of Greek political thought, a practical demonstration of citizen autonomy, fundamental to democracy (Hdt. 5.78.1) but also conveying an acceptance of rigid social structures in which character fits a person to a class, as in Plato's principle of specialization (Plato *Rep.* 2.369b–70c, 4.433a4–6).

Ischomachus draws a parallel between the job of managing a hive and that of managing the house:

I think that the female leader (*hēgemōn*) of the bees practises tasks of this kind, set in place for her by the god.

   'What tasks does the queen bee (*basilissa*) have that resemble the work which I must do?' she said.   (*Oec.* 7.32)

He goes on to explain that the queen ensures that worker bees are working, sending them out on missions, and storing and eventually distributing what they bring in, in well-ordered honeycombs. Rearing the next generation of enslaved workers is also her responsibility (7.33–4), as is sending the workforce out on their tasks (7.35). The bee and the hive were a traditional image for an orderly society, present in Homer and other authors, and the 'bee woman' is, in the otherwise entirely negative taxonomy of women presented by the iambic poet Semonides, the ideal wife.[25] Ischomachus imagines that his young wife might enjoy teaching slaves to spin, but be wearied by taking care of them when they are sick (*Oec.* 7.37, 41). The emphasis on the wife's caring oversight (*epimeleia*) and her ability to transmit knowledge show that her role is integrated into Xenophon's Socratic value system, even though Ischomachus' wife perceptively notes that her leadership role will be perceived as

---

[24] On the *nomos*/*physis* opposition, see Lloyd 1966: 124–5; on its use in the discussion of justice, see Bonazzi 2020: 65–95.

[25] Hom. *Il.* 2.87–93; Semonides fr. 7.84–94; see Osborne 2001 on Semonides' sympotic context. Xenophon uses the queen bee image again (*Cyr.* 5.1.24), in a masculine, Persian context (Brock 2004: 254).

laughable compared with that of her husband and his external-facing activities (7.39).[26]

Within the house, however, the wife is a ruler, a 'queen' (*basilissa*). The maintenance of domestic order becomes the wife's prime duty:

> In addition to all these points, Socrates, I said to my wife that there was no benefit in all these arrangements, unless she herself took care (*epimelēsetai*) that good order (*taxis*) was kept for each object. I taught her that in cities with good laws (*eunomoumenais polesin*) the citizens thought that it was not enough to write good laws, but they also elected guardians of the law (*nomophulakas*), who acted as overseers and praised who acted lawfully, and punished anyone who acted contrary to the law.   (*Oec.* 9.14–15)

Reflection and self-examination are part of this order, in which the well-run household is likened to a city 'with good laws', a quality that Athenians attributed to Sparta.[27] Ischomachus hears his wife's comments on his actions, with slaves and others acting as if the household had political institutions:

> 'We often deliberate about the actions we plan to take, and speak in praise of these, while we criticize those actions we do not want to do. Indeed, Socrates,' he said, 'I have often been judged and convicted to suffer some punishment or pay a fine.'
> 'By whom, Ischomachus?' I asked. 'I can't work it out.'
> 'By my wife,' he said.   (*Oec.* 11.24–5)

The idea of a domestic law court might also suggest comic scenarios such as that of Aristophanes' *Wasps*.[28] The comedic potential has led to suggestions that the whole presentation of Ischomachus and his wife is ironic, pointing to the story of Chrysilla, the widow of the historical Ischomachus, whose far from ideal behaviour is reported by the speechwriter Andocides (*On the Mysteries* 122–4).[29] On this reading, the *Oeconomicus* offers a critique of the idea of the *kalos kagathos* and delusions of good order. But the inclusion of so many key ethical ideas in these passages makes a wholly ironic reading difficult. Xenophon is committed to these views on good social order elsewhere in his work, and the fact that he regards a woman as capable of

---

[26] Care: ἐπιμελεῖται 7.34; ἐπιμελητέον 36; ἐπιμελημάτων, ἐπιμελητέον 37; ἐπιμελοῖο 39; ἐπιμέλειαι 41. Knowledge: προνοητέον 36, ἐπιστήμονα 41.

[27] Cf. the *nomophulakes* of Plato's Magnesia, introduced at Pl. *Leg.* 6.752d.

[28] Pomeroy 1994 does not make this link, but David Johnson (2021: 226) compares the *Symposium* with *Wasps*.

[29] This Chrysilla, after the death of her husband, moved in with her daughter and became the mistress of her son-in-law Callias, the same Callias who is the host of Xenophon's *Symposium*. See Davies 1971: 265–8 and Nails 2002: 94–95; with further analysis from Hobden 2017: 168–73 and Johnson 2021: 269–73.

implementing them in a specific domain is, as Sheila Murnaghan observed, to treat women's roles as 'emphatically equal' and 'complementary' to the role of the man in other forms of ordered social arrangement.[30] Ischomachus grants that his wife, in having this ability, has a 'great-thinking' (*megalaphrona*) mind; after completing his description of her skill in prudent household management, all expressed in language more usually linked to men's roles, he accepts Socrates' remark on her 'masculine mentality' (*andrikēn...dianoian*, 10.1).

However, Ischomachus undercuts his positive assessment by his next point.[31] Xenophon uses him to idealize marriage as a relationship of total frankness, including honest self-presentation. When his wife wears make-up and built-up shoes, Ischomachus claims that her altered appearance precludes any real connection or frank communication between them (10.2–13). His wife makes no verbal reply to his criticism, but Ischomachus notes:

> She never did anything of this kind again after this, but tried to display herself with a clean (*katharan*) and suitable (*prepontōs*) appearance. However, she did ask me how she might appear beautiful (*kalē*) in reality (*tōi onti*) and not only seem to be so.
>
> (*Oec.* 10.9)

We might note the philosophical language Xenophon gives the unnamed wife. As he alludes to contemporary philosophical discussions of the difference between appearance and reality, he emphasizes the importance of honesty in relationships, and the distinction between virtue and vice.[32] Ischomachus' wife appears to have become fluent in the technical language of Socratic dialogue, and in the Platonic distinction between reality and appearance.

Ischomachus explains that she should display her true nature by distinguishing herself from her slaves through her active working stance at the loom (10.10). While Xenophon has an abiding interest in the self-presentation of individuals performing leadership roles, there is no scope for the positive use of self-adornment in the private life of an Athenian wife.[33] The distinction of citizen from slave carries further

---

[30] Murnaghan 1988: 9; Baragwanath forthcoming.

[31] Socrates' reference to the painter Zeuxis links this discussion to the appearance of his rival Parrhasius in *Mem.* 3.10.1–5.

[32] Xenophon's insistence that character can be apprehended by sight (*Mem.* 3.10) contrasts with the Platonic deprecation of direct perception of the material world in favour of intellection of the Forms (*Rep.* 5–6, especially 5.476b; lovers of sights and sounds).

[33] See Chapter 6 for Xenophon's thought on the self-presentation of monarchs.

into the personal lives of the couple. Ischomachus maps the distinction between the self-presentation and activity of the citizen wife and the enslaved woman on to the virtue/vice distinction: 'Her appearance generates sexual desire, when she, with her cleaner appearance and more appropriate clothing is compared with a slave, and above all when she grants favours willingly, rather than being compelled to give service' (*Oec.* 10.12–13). While other sexual partners are available for Athenian husbands – their own domestic slaves, as suggested here, and sex workers of various types – only the citizen wife represents Virtue. In parallel with political typologies of good and bad regimes, her willing submission to her husband's desire makes his domination acceptable.

Xenophon's characters have differing attitudes to domestic resources being expended on the pursuit of sexual pleasure. Socrates criticizes the expenditure which would be involved in maintaining a relationship with *hetairai* like Theodote, who were maintained by one or more customers who regarded them as 'friends' but paid them substantial sums for the privilege of doing so: 'If someone were to use his money to buy a sexual partner, through which he would become worse in both body and soul, and worse in respect of his estate, how would money actually be beneficial for him?' (*Oec* 1.13). The reality, however, was that many Athenian men made use of sex workers; Antisthenes implies that doing so on a casual basis meets his physical need for sex (*Symp.* 4.38). Xenophon also considers the perspective of the sex workers themselves, although with some subtle criticism. The enslaved entertainers of the *Symposium* vote Critobulus to be more beautiful than Socrates (*Symp.* 5.9), emphasizing that they are concerned with the physical and external rather than the internal beauty of the soul.

Socrates' encounter with the beautiful *hetaira* Theodote (*Mem.* 3.11) provides a view of an Athenian household headed not by a male citizen but by a female non-citizen. When Theodote surprises him by addressing him directly as he and his companions discuss her beauty, Socrates questions Theodote to discover the source of her income.[34] She does not benefit from revenue from farming or property – indeed, as a non-citizen she is not able to own land or real property outright – but is dependent on gifts from friends. Socrates' probing questions establish that she has no strategy for attracting the customers on whom she depends. In a further animal image, he compares her with

---

[34] See Goldhill 1998; Atack 2024.

a spider which can weave a web but has no strategy to drive prey into its trap (3.11.5–7).

Spartan arrangements contrast with those of Athens. Xenophon begins the *Lacedaimonion politeia* with an account of citizen women's domestic lives in Sparta and their role in producing the next generation. Compared with women elsewhere, Spartan young women enjoy better food, and are permitted more exercise, so are in a better physical condition, conducive to the production of healthier children, which is their eventual primary function (*LP* 1.3–10).[35] Domestic labour such as the production of clothing is the work of the enslaved. Social norms limit the time a man may spend at home and reduce opportunities for marital intercourse, again in the interests of the production of better children, and men are encouraged to marry and father children while at their physical peak. In Xenophon's account eugenic considerations about the size and strength of offspring outweigh concerns about marital fidelity, and Lycurgus' *politeia* permitted older men's wives to bear children for younger men other than their husbands.[36] As Noreen Humble notes, this discussion is introduced and closed with invitations to the reader to consider the question; Xenophon's concern may be as much to offer a counter-example to Athenian norms as to explore Spartan society.[37] Given the centrality of the household in his thought, he may not have embraced Sparta's physical separation of male and female spheres.

Xenophon pays more attention to the reality of women's lives than Plato does, and appears to grant women more epistemic and moral agency and capability than Aristotle does in *Politics* Book 1, a work which in many places appears to look back to Xenophon's thought on the household. But his mapping of the characteristics of virtue and vice on to two different modes of performing a female gender identity shows that he is still enmeshed within the patriarchal structures and binaries of Athenian culture.

---

[35] Compare the depiction of the physically active Spartan woman Lampito at Ar. *Lys*. 78–84.
[36] Cartledge 1981.
[37] Humble 2022: 97.

The lives and work of the enslaved

Xenophon rarely focuses on enslaved individuals themselves, but enslavement as a status is central to his thought.[38] He differentiates the roles of enslaved workers, and notes the skill with which some might themselves perform supervisory roles within and outside the home (*Oec.* 12.3–20; *Mem.* 2.5.2). However, his references to the enslaved are most often embedded in political analogies in which their status becomes a metaphor for the political unfreedom of citizens, his primary concern. As seen in the contrast between free and enslaved women in the *Oeconomicus*, the enslaved and the free come to represent binary oppositions between bad and good epistemic and moral states. Enslavement further becomes a metaphor for domination by the drive for pleasure. Xenophon describes men who lack control over their physical appetites:

These too are slaves (*douloi*), and they are ruled by extremely harsh masters…when they perceive that they are unable to work because of age, they abandon them to a wretched old age and try to use others as their slaves, in turn. But, Critobulus, we must constantly fight for our freedom (*eleutherias*) against these influences even more than against armed men trying to enslave us (*katadoulousthai*). (*Oec.* 1.22–3)

The analogical enslavement to vice of a free person is in Xenophon's account a more significant matter than the lived experience of personal enslavement. A further consequence is that the negative qualities associated with enslavement through analogy are transferred to enslaved persons themselves, who are then viewed as inherently vicious through being subject to base desires (*Mem.* 1.2.29, 1.3.11). Such views underlie Aristotle's theory of natural slavery (*Pol.* 1.5–6), in which individuals can be identified as naturally suited to the status of enslavement. Xenophon's thought may well contribute to this model.[39]

Xenophon does, however, recognize the economic value of the enslaved to the household and to its business enterprises, through their skilled and even specialist labour. His recommendations for the management of Athenian public finance in the *Poroi* effectively turn the city into a large household, exploiting its enslaved workers to boost production of silver (*Poroi* 4.2–4, 13–26).[40]

[38] Baragwanath 2012.
[39] See Atack forthcoming. On Aristotle's thought on enslavement, see Schofield 1990.
[40] See Chapter 4.

Within Ischomachus' house, enslaved workers are overseen by his wife, and kept separated by sex, with the door to the women's quarters kept locked so that the enslaved will not 'produce children without our assent' (*Oec.* 9.5). Outside in the fields, he trains labourers and supervisors in agricultural work, believing it important that a master demonstrate his good qualities and concern (*epimeleia*) for his workers:

When the master provides an example of neglect (*amelein*), it is difficult for a servant to become careful (*epimelē*); to summarize, I think I have never observed good slaves of a bad master, and though I have seen bad slaves of a good master, they certainly did not go unpunished.   (*Oec.* 12.18–19)

Although owner and enslaved are both part of the household, Xenophon assumes that there will often be conflict between them; this is another way in which the household offers an analogy for class conflict within the *polis*. Socrates notes that, in some households, the enslaved are kept in chains, yet still keep running away, whereas in others they stay despite a lack of physical restraint (*Oec.* 3.4). Xenophon connects brutality towards the enslaved with a lack of order in the arrangement of belongings (*Oec.* 3.2). Here again the household is seen as a microcosm of larger-scale communities, in which those who rule over willing subjects are more successful as rulers (*Cyr.* 1.1.5–6; *Hiero* 11.12–15).[41]

Xenophon's portrait of the hedonist Aristippus makes the connection between being a slave-owner and rejecting the idea of community and necessary concessions to its demands. A slave-owner himself, he regards life as a citizen, subjected to the rule of others, as equivalent to life as an enslaved worker (*Mem.* 2.1.11). Xenophon subtly portrays the hypocrisy embedded in this equation, while laying out the brutal treatment the enslaved might expect, as Socrates points out the inconsistencies in his argument:

'Or is it because you realize that a man like you would be of no use as a slave to any master? Who would want a man in his household who is averse to hard work and takes his pleasure in the most expensive living?

'And let's look at how masters treat slaves like that. Don't they suppress their sexual urges by starving them, stop them from stealing by locking away anything they could take, and beat the laziness out of them with floggings? Or what action do you yourself take when you realize that you have a slave of that sort in your house?'

---

[41] Note the use of the use of the same word (*despotēs*) for the head of household and tyrannical ruler. See Arist. *Eth. Nic.* 8.10.1160b27–30.

'I punish him hard in every way,' he said, 'until I force him to do what a slave should.'
(*Mem.* 2.1.15–17)

Aristippus' comments betray the reality of enslavement, as does a further discussion with Antisthenes on the value of skilled enslaved workers.

'Tell me, Antisthenes,' he said, 'do friends have various values in the same way that domestic slaves do? One slave is worth perhaps two minas, another not even half a mina, another five minas, and another ten: and they say that Nicias the son of Niceratus paid a whole talent for a manager of his silver mines. So I'm interested in the answer to this – do friends vary in value in the same way as slaves?' (*Mem.* 2.5.2)

Xenophon shows that slaves have a measurable market value, easily assessed according to their skills, but that it is difficult to work out the financial value of friends. Both good slaves and friends bring financial benefits and, as the discussion concludes, the former should not be sold and the latter not abandoned (2.5.5).

Homosociality: men's personal relationships outside the home

Book 2 of the *Memorabilia* shows how citizen men articulate their house-holds' relationship with other households and with the city through a range of relationships, from formal affiliation through demes (administrative neighbourhoods), cults, and shared military experience, to informal networks of friendship. Friendship between citizens thus has both a personal and a political aspect.[42] Xenophon's account suggests directions which foreshadow Aristotle's typology of citizen friendship (Books 8 and 9 of the *Nicomachean Ethics*).[43] Such relationships cement the unity of the citizen body. Xenophon also attempts to integrate a further form of extra-familial male relationship – pederastic relationships between young adults and youths – into his longer investigation of friendship (*Mem.* 2.6), perhaps as a critical comment on the role such relationships play in Plato's dialogues. For Xenophon, erotic relationships between young men risk the loss of physical and mental self-control.

Friendship begins with family members, who offer the first line of defence for the citizen against the competitive environment of the wider *polis*. When Chaerecrates is struggling to get on with his brother

---

[42] On friendship in the classical polis, see Konstan 1997: 53–92.
[43] On Aristotle's models of friendship, see J. Cooper 1977; Price 1997; Schofield 1998.

Chaerephon (Socrates' good friend, who appears in Aristophanes' *Clouds* and Plato's *Apology*),[44] Socrates advises him on improving this vital relationship, and emphasizes the importance of family bonds:

> Again, people who can afford it buy slaves to assist them in the house, and acquire friends for the help they can give, but ignore their brothers – as if they can develop friendships with their fellow citizens, but not with their brothers. And yet common parentage and growing up together are powerful factors making for friendship, as can be seen in the instinctive sense of loss which even animals feel when they miss the siblings who shared their nurture.   (*Mem.* 2.3.3–4)

Brothers, who will defend each other, are less likely to come under attack in their citizen life.

The family is the closest source of support for a citizen, but wider networks are also needed. Friendship (*philia*) properly extends across a wide range of citizen interactions beyond the household and immediate family. Acquiring friends from outside the family was important in building a network of mutual benefit; Xenophon treats this as a kind of property transaction, resulting in friendship being a social good with an exchange value.[45] Socrates emphasizes this to an unnamed interlocutor (*Mem.* 2.4): friends help by providing practical support in both public and private matters, filling gaps in provision, and even joining in physical defence. Friends are also sources of personal and emotional support. The quality of friends contributes to their value (2.4.5–7).

In a subsequent conversation with Antisthenes, Socrates develops the monetary valuation of friendship. He concludes that, 'just as someone will put an unsatisfactory slave on the market for what he will fetch, so it may be tempting to sell an unsatisfactory friend when there is the possibility of gaining more than he is worth' (2.5.7). Friends fit into networks of exchange, both as providers and recipients of immaterial goods, *charis*, or favours and prestige, and as possessions themselves in the exchange of actual money and goods. Xenophon's assessment of them as objects of value seems crass, but he is simply extending ideas current in political theorizing about the need for an exchange rate between citizens who contribute different amounts, expressed in the concept of 'geometric' equality.[46]

---

[44] Ar. *Nub.* 144–7, 156; Pl. *Ap.* 20e–21a; Moore 2013: 286–7.
[45] Azoulay 2018b.
[46] Most fully explored in Arist. *Eth. Nic.* 5.5; see Harvey 1965.

Xenophon develops this idea further in Socrates' long conversation with his favoured interlocutor Critobulus, the son of his own friend Crito (*Mem.* 2.6), and the interlocutor of the *Oeconomicus*. Socrates advises his young friend pragmatically, to seek friends who exhibit self-control over their physical appetites, who possess financial prudence, and who do not come with a network of enemies. Yet, despite the evident monetary calculus, a friend who loves money would be a bad choice (*Mem.* 2.6.3–4).

Possible friends should be sought out and pursued, a process Xenophon describes using management of the enslaved and the aristocratic pastime of hunting as an analogy, as he later does for the courtesan Theodote's pursuit of 'friends':

Well, it's certainly not by chasing him on foot like a hare, or trapping him with snares like a bird, or using brute force on him as we would on an enemy. It is hard work to capture a friend against his will, and difficult to keep him tied up like a slave. That sort of treatment turns people into enemies rather than friends.   (*Mem.* 2.6.9)

Socrates goes on to liken the personal pursuit of friends to politicians' pursuit of supporters. So prominent figures like Pericles and Themistocles (2.6.13), who are able to attract support, through either fair means or some kind of enchantment, offer one model for finding friends. Taking the analogy in the other direction, Socrates adds that politicians gain support from flatterers, but that such men are unsuitable as friends. He notes the importance of friends sharing in good personal qualities, restating an analogy between the pursuit of friends and the pursuit of lovers:

Perhaps I myself could use my expertise in matters of love (*erōtikos*) to help you in that hunt for men of quality. When I want someone, it's quite something how completely I throw myself into getting him to reciprocate my love (*antiphileisthai*), my longing for him, my desire for his company. I see that you too will need this passion when you want to form friendships.   (*Mem.* 2.6.28–9)

Critobulus expresses a wish for help with the pursuit of beautiful young men as an actual form of friendship, collapsing the analogy. Affective and erotic relationships between men and youths were a special class of citizen relationship, one of some anxiety to Athenian society, even as they played an important role in the acculturation of elite youths into adult social practices.[47] Xenophon follows Plato's treatment of

---

[47] Compare Aeschines, *Against Timarchus*; see Fisher 1992; Lear 2015; Atack 2021.

these relationships in the context of friendship (*Lysis* 212b1–2), as Melina Tamiolaki notes.[48]

Xenophon expresses concern about the effect of pederastic relationships, but his concern is for the well-being of the older party, centred on the loss of physical and mental self-control demonstrated by falling in love and expressing longing for the younger 'beloved'. Unusually, he depicts himself in conversation with Socrates, who criticizes those who lose self-control in their enthusiastic pursuit of beautiful youths (*Mem.* 1.3.8–13). The speech is really aimed at Critobulus, who has kissed the beautiful son of Alcibiades; Xenophon admits that he would have done the same:

'You poor man,' said Socrates, 'and what do you think would happen to you after kissing a beauty like that? Wouldn't you at that very instant become a slave (*doulos*) rather than a free agent (*eleutherou*), and then spend loads of money on debilitating pleasures, have no time at all to devote to anything fine and good, and find yourself forced to take an interest in things to which no-one, not even a madman (*mainomenos*), would pay any attention?'   (*Mem.* 1.3.11)

Again, the loss of self-control involved in erotic pursuit is likened to enslavement and madness, the loss of reason. However, Xenophon differs from Plato in his rejection of any physical aspect within these relationships.[49] Critias is criticized for rubbing himself against a boy 'like a pig' (1.2.30), behaviour more suited to the unfree (*aneleutheron*) than to the *kalos kagathos* gentleman (1.2.29), who has learned to control his physical appetites.

Xenophon's treatment of homosocial and homoerotic relationships reacts to Plato's erotic dialogues; *Mem* 2.6 responds closely to Plato's *Lysis*.[50] Relationships between men are the focus of Xenophon's *Symposium*, which replies to Plato's work of the same name, and offers a subtle and witty critique of Plato's presentation of *eros* and of the role of pederasty in Socratic thought.[51] In Xenophon's work, Socrates and his companions are invited to join what might seem a rather awkward party, at which the host, Callias, is pursuing Autolycus, the son of his guest Lycon. The occasion for the event is Autolycus' victory in an all-in wrestling contest (*pankration*, *Symp.* 8.37). Both Callias and Autolycus are still just about young enough to engage in pederastic

---

[48] Tamiolaki 2018; Berkel 2020: 263–329.
[49] Plato (*Phdr.*, *Symp.*) is not entirely consistent on this point.
[50] Hobden 2005; Tamiolaki 2018.
[51] Huss 1999b; Johnson 2021: 187–230; Baragwanath and Verity 2022; Gilhuly 2024.

relationships, although the hazy dramatic setting pays no attention to chronology. Through this set-up, Socrates analogizes his own activities to matchmaking, pimping, and erotic pursuit (*Symp.* 8.42).

Critobulus' own beauty opens a discussion and contest between him and Socrates; the symposiasts acknowledge Socrates' inner beauty, while the enslaved entertainers brought by a Sicilian impresario vote for the handsome young man (*Symp.* 5.9). The Sicilian in turn becomes annoyed that the guests are entertaining themselves and ignoring the dancers' performances, and Socrates' presence is resented by the interloper Philippus, who eventually launches into a critique which mirrors the later accusations against Socrates, in which Lycon was the third prosecutor (6.6–10).

When Socrates intervenes to put the party back on track, he encourages the other guests to sing, while asking the entertainers to dance (7.1).[52] His closing speech (8.12–41) encourages Callias to pursue a chaste friendship with Autolycus rather than a sexual relationship, and he argues that non-sexual relationships between men offer a route to virtue for both parties:

For the greatest good for the man who yearns to make a good friend from his boyfriend is that it is necessary that he too should practise virtue. For it is not possible for a man who performs shameful deeds to produce a companion who is good, nor can a man who exhibits shamelessness and lack of self-control make his beloved show self-control and respect.   (*Symp.* 8.26)

While criticizing Pausanias' admiration of the Theban Sacred Band, 150 pairs of lovers who fought side by side (8.32), Xenophon appears to acknowledge Pausanias' relationship with the poet Agathon. In doing so, he sets his work in conversation with Plato's *Symposium*, from which the female performers were excluded.[53]

However, the dancers' final scene, representing an erotic encounter between Dionysus and Ariadne, provides a reminder of the allure of heterosexual love within citizen marriage (9.2–5). Autolycus leaves with his father, while the other married guests rush home to their wives (*Symp.* 9.7). While male friendship is central to existence in the city, the household and the wife within it have an importance for Xenophon not shared by Plato.

---

[52] Huss 1999a.
[53] Danzig 2005, Pl. *Smp.* 176e, 178e (Phaedrus' speech).

The Athenian gentleman on his estate and in the *agora*

Just as Xenophon has a clear view of the proper role of women in maintaining their households, he outlines the behaviour and activity appropriate to citizen men who are heads of households and responsible for what might be substantial estates. The political and legal duties of a citizen towards the *polis* might appear as a disruption to this core responsibility, as seen in the routine of Ischomachus, presented as the supreme example of the 'fine and good' gentleman, the *kalos kagathos* (*Oec.* 7.2–3).[54]

Physical self-improvement was a key task for the gentleman. Ischomachus explains how his daily routine contributes to a regime of fitness and the care of self and others:

> Well now, Socrates, I'm in the habit of getting out of bed when I might find others still indoors, if I need to meet anyone. If I have anything to do down in the city, in conducting this business I take the opportunity for a walk. And if there's no business in town, my slave leads my horse to the field, but I take a walk on the path to the field, and it's probably better, Socrates, than if I were to walk in the arcade. When I reach the field, if they are planting or clearing or sowing or reaping the harvest, I look closely at how each task is being done and suggest improvements, if I have anything better than their present method. After this I typically mount my horse and practise horsemanship (*hippasian*), as like as I can make it to the cavalry functions needed in warfare...   (*Oec.* 11.14–17)

Ischomachus' involvement with farming is a supervisory one, although, as he and Socrates observe, supervision requires a knowledge of the tasks being supervised. His key task is to train the managers who take care of farming for him and directly manage his workforce. Socrates is somewhat sceptical that such supervisory skills can be taught, as Ischomachus insists (12.4). This point keys into a significant debate about the teachability of virtue, seen in Plato's dialogues.[55]

Although Ischomachus' manager is enslaved, like those he manages, Xenophon suggests that a citizen who had fallen into poverty might take up the work of an estate manager rather than labouring work (*Mem.* 2.8.3). Eutherus has lost his own property, and his best option for income is day labouring in the city, as unpropertied free citizens did. But, Socrates suggests, working for the owner of a large estate would

---

[54] For an exhaustive survey, see Bourriot 1995.
[55] See Pl. *Meno* 70a–73d; *Lach.* 190bd; *Prt.* 323c–328a.

not involve physical labour. It would, however, challenge Eutherus' ideas about what activities are appropriate for a free citizen:

'I would find it hard, Socrates,' he said, 'to submit to the condition of a slave (*douleian*).'

'And yet those who take charge of their cities and supervise public affairs are not regarded as thereby lowering themselves to the status of a slave (*douloprepesteroi*), but rather as displaying more of the qualities of a free man (*eleutheriōteroi*).' (*Mem.* 2.8.4)

One of the problems introduced by identifying the rule and management of a household with that of the *polis* is that in Athens the two tasks were undertaken by people of different statuses: office-holders in the city were free citizens, whereas stewards in private households might well be enslaved. The aristocratic idea that subjection to the will of the majority was a form of enslavement, most clearly voiced by Aristippus (see Chapter 4), also impacts the idea that working for another citizen in his private business was not a suitable task for a free citizen.

A further division among Athenian citizens was between those who undertook civic roles and played an active part in the administration of the city, and those who kept a low profile and focused on their private affairs.[56] Ischomachus appears to adopt a quietist attitude, and to avoid public entanglement in politics; some have argued that this implicates Xenophon in an oligarchic perspective.[57] Socrates argues against this notion, encouraging Charmides, something of a real-life Ischomachus, to take a more active role in civic affairs, and re-emphasizing the view that managing household and city are the same function. Socrates tells him he has an obligation to use his skills for the public good, but Charmides insists that his private abilities are not transferable to the public sphere:[58]

Charmides replied, 'Conversation in private is not the same as debate in a crowded assembly, Socrates.'

'And yet', said Socrates, 'anyone who can count is able to count just as well in front of a crowd as on his own, and the best lyre-players in the privacy of their home are also the best in public performance.'   (*Mem.* 3.7.4)

---

[56] Carter 1986.
[57] See L. Strauss 1970; Pangle 2020: 77–84.
[58] Johnson 2021: 259–60.

There is a balance in Ischomachus' activities between farming on his estate and transacting commercial business in the marketplace or with fellow citizens. One might expect a *kalos kagathos* to favour farming over trade. David Johnson suggests that Ischomachus' business activities and views may mark him as a less than perfect exemplar of a conventional gentleman.[59] Xenophon certainly appreciates the Spartan prohibition of citizen participation in trade (*LP* 7.1–3), and his contemporaries shared such views. Plato largely disdains the financial sphere, forbidding property to his philosopher rulers, while Aristotle's *Politics* polices a line between good citizen behaviour and interest in profit-seeking and money matters (*chrēmatistikē*, *Pol.* 1.10.1258a18–25).[60] Yet Ischomachus points out that grain traders love the produce they trade just as much as farmers do (*Oec.* 20.27–9).

Matthew Christ, by contrast, suggests that Xenophon is arguing against an aristocratic ideology of non-participation, by showing that the skills of good estate management, exemplified by Ischomachus (and also by Charmides), should benefit the city and earn honours for those who possess them.[61] Xenophon, he contends, shows 'a new vision of elite identity' in which hard work in managing private business benefits the public standing of the elite, and successful estate management is achieved through cooperation with democratic processes and participation in office-holding. Xenophon attributes a similar view – that the *kalos kagathos* should provide the necessities for his household – to the Persian king Cambyses (*Cyr.* 1.6.7). Such activity should be supported by relevant expertise; the later sections of the *Oeconomicus* provide detailed instruction on farming practice for producing and harvesting crops (*Oec.* 15.10–19.19). By setting Socrates' and Ischomachus' conversation in the *agora*, where business was undertaken, rather than in a private setting, Xenophon underlines Ischomachus' commitment to taking charge of his business affairs, and also aligns him with Socrates' practice of public conversation. Ischomachus' international perspective may also be unusual. As well as his praise for Persian leaders as farmers (*Oec.* 4.4), his model of good order is a Phoenician trading ship (*Oec.* 8.11–16).

While elite Athenian women's responsibilities were largely restricted to their households, other than the performance of religious ritual

---

[59] Johnson 2021: 234.
[60] On Plato, Xenophon, and business, see Ober 2022: 295–344.
[61] Christ 2020: 97–101.

outside the home, men's lives required social and political interaction in other venues, both through formal institutions and through informal friendship networks. Xenophon has firm views on the proper leisure activities through which *kaloi kagathoi* could demonstrate their status and maintain their skills and physical fitness, valorizing these efforts as labour (*ponos*), which he contrasts with the physical work of lower-class citizens and the enslaved, which damages rather than improves.[62] Simply having the time and resources for leisure marked the elite as superior to propertyless wage-labourers; whatever form their non-productive activity took, from *symposia* in the city to hunting in the countryside, it demonstrated their status and command of expensive resources, and their ability to build relationships through bestowing generosity (*charis*).[63]

In the countryside, hunting was an important leisure pursuit for the elite, and could play a part in preparing young men for military service: 'Those who are keen on this pursuit will benefit in many ways. For it furnishes health for their bodies, keener sight and hearing, slower ageing, and above all educates in matters of war' (*Cyn.* 12.1–2). The practical benefits of hunting include fitness, better horsemanship (elite men rode to the hunt, but the actual hunting was done on foot with the assistance of slaves), and experience of roughing it – all useful for military life. Further benefits include the development of character virtues, because hunting required cooperation between hunters in the pursuit of prey and driving it into nets, and the sharing of resources including both equipment and trained hounds (as practised in Sparta, according to *LP* 6.3).

Xenophon has a great deal of detailed comment to make on the breeding and management of hounds, the most important resource needed for hunting hares, a typical activity in Attica (*Cyn.* 3–4, 6–7).[64] Yet the *Cynegeticus* ranges far beyond the practicalities of keeping hounds and training support staff for this purpose. It considers the hunting of larger animals: the wild boar of heroic hunting (10.1–23) and, briefly, the large cats and bears found far beyond Greece (11.1–4). Fishing and trapping birds for subsistence or trade ('night-hunting', 12.7) was not valorized in the same way; as with other activities, the distinction between elite and non-elite forms serves to further link

---

[62] Loraux 1982; Johnstone 1994.
[63] Azoulay 2018a: 73–6.
[64] See Phillips and Willcock 1999.

the non-elite with the enslaved.[65] Xenophon concludes with the claim that hunting contributes to the development of desirable qualities in the *kalos kagathos* (12.1–9), against those who argue that it is an indulgence.

Conclusion

The household is central to Xenophon's model of organization and rule, both as the site in which individuals develop and live cooperatively, and as a miniature example of hierarchy through which virtue can flow from top to bottom. His focus on the household enables him to grant women as household managers some capacity to organize, lead, and exhibit virtue. He also pays great attention to the personal relationships, within and beyond families, which negotiate the interrelationship of household and city, showing how friendships of different sorts, including pederasty, bring citizens together, including into each other's homes. But citizens also interact outside their homes, and do not always agree. The next chapter explores Xenophon's thought on the city as a collectivity of individuals and households.

---

[65] Compare Pl. *Leg.* 8.822d–824a.

IV. THE CITY

Although Xenophon spent much of his adult life living outside Athens and the *polis* framework, Athens itself and the city as the basis for achieving the good life were central to his thought, both philosophical and practical. He keenly observed the practices of other communities, especially Sparta, long a source of fascination for Athens' elite.[1] He compared the impact of different customs and forms of rule on cities such as Sparta (*Constitution of the Lacedaimonians, Agesilaus*), Syracuse (*Hiero*), and his imagined Persia and Babylon (*Cyropaedia*). Some of his thought on constructing political communities is contained in his *politeia* texts (*LP*; *Cyr.* 1.2), but his most sustained and systematic engagement with the topic is through Socrates' conversations with Athenians in Book 3 of the *Memorabilia*.

In both real and imagined contexts, Xenophon highlights the difficulties of civic elites living up to the expectations placed on them, and the punishments suffered by Athenian generals whose performance in the field displeased the democracy. The latter ranged from dismissal and fines (Timotheus, *Hell.* 6.2.10–13; see Chapter 5) to execution (the Arginusae generals, *Hell.* 1.6–7). He criticizes the tendency of Athenian and other democracies to punish their leaders, arguing that it operates as a disincentive to elite participation in governance (*Hell.* 1.7, *Mem.* 3.1–7). He also criticizes the fickleness of the *dēmos*, while showing how sophistic discourse had subverted the elite's commitment to social unity, typified by his representation of Alcibiades' criticism of Pericles' attempts to define law (*Mem.* 1.2.40–6, discussed below; see also *Cyn.* 13.1–9).[2]

Despite his own experiences, Xenophon argues strongly that political participation is a necessary duty for the elite male citizen, who realizes his potential for excellence by benefiting his community. He treats the education of the young, their first experiences outside their home, as vital for the formation of political community. He has Socrates criticize the hedonist Aristippus for arguing against political participation (*Mem.* 2.1). The idea that the majority might oppress the minority ran counter to the Greek ideal of *homonoia*, consensus and unanimity among the citizen body, an ideal which Xenophon shared (*Mem.* 4.4.16). He

---

[1] See e.g. Ar. *Vesp.* 462–76; Critias fr. DK 88 B6, 34–7. See also Bonazzi 2020: 133–4.
[2] On the *Cynegeticus* passage, see L'Allier 2008.

also addresses questions of inequality between citizens, and the just distribution of reward and honour, but in the context of Cyrus' Persian army rather than Athens itself (*Cyr.* 2.1–4).

Xenophon uses existing typologies and structures to characterize political regimes in terms of the number of persons exercising rule: one, few, or many. He sees good and bad versions of regime types, especially monarchy. He values stability and consensus (*homonoia*), seeing regimes which achieved them as aligned with the divine ordering of the world (*eukosmia*; *Cyr.* 1.2.4, 8.1.33).[3] For Xenophon, such regimes are those outside Athens: Cyrus' Persian empire and Sparta in the past. One problem with Athenian democracy, as he sees it, is that mass participation and debate has led to division and faction, along class lines, eliminating the possibility of consensus and effectively tyrannizing the elite minority. Another is that free citizens have to submit to the rule of office-holders, a situation casually analogized to enslavement in the discussion between Socrates and Aristippus (*Mem.* 2.1.8–17).

Xenophon's political language suggests that he is addressing readers sympathetic with a conservative and anti-democratic perspective. In both historical and philosophical works he refers to the *dēmos* as an *ochlos* ('mob'), and a *plēthos* ('number', 'mass', sometimes 'majority'), less pejorative but also dehumanizing.[4]

Preparing the next generation: Socrates and other educators

Unlike Plato, Aristotle, and Isocrates, Xenophon was not a professional educator; while he is deeply concerned with the education of the next generation, his critique of educators does not arise from a personal stake in the business of teaching. He believes that education can develop cohesion among the governing class, and therefore that the education of civic leaders should be managed by the city itself rather than left to private family arrangements, as was the case in Athens (*LP* 2.2). He praises Sparta's arrangements, which he ascribes to the lawgiver Lycurgus, for preparing its elite male citizens for their military

---

[3] See Chapter 6.

[4] *Ochlos*: *Hell.* 1.3.22, 1.4.13, 1.7.13, 2.2.21, 3.3.7, 3.4.7, 4.4.8, 11, 6.2.33, 6.4.14; *Mem.* 1.1.14, 3.7.5; *Symp.* 2.18, 8.5; *Cyr.* 2.2.21, 7.5.39; *Hiero* 2.3, 6.4; and frequently in the *Anabasis* to refer to the camp followers. *plēthos* referring to the *dēmos*, in a pejorative sense: *Hell.* 1.7.12, 5.2.32; *Mem.* 1.2.43. On Xenophon's sympathy with democracy, see Gray 2011c; Christ 2020.

role, and he assigns a similar set of institutions to Persia. The idea that education, at least for future leaders, was a collective or social responsibility was shared by Plato, seen in his idealized arrangements for Kallipolis (*Republic*) and Magnesia (*Laws*).

Xenophon's educational ideal is evident in the arrangements he describes in his Persian *politeia*. The state education provided in the Persian *agora* is available only to a subset of boys from elite families who can pay for it (*Cyr.* 1.2.15), although it is a necessary qualification for holding office. That education is focused on learning about justice, as a key societal value (1.3.16–17), but also on developing both personal qualities of self-control, and military skills through physical education (1.2.6–8). Boys learn to manage their physical appetites through communal dining overseen by their teachers. Older youths learn additional skills through hunting practice, and from training sessions when they are not hunting.

In describing this educational regime, Xenophon draws on his knowledge of the Spartan education system, which he praises in his *Constitution of the Spartans* (*LP* 2.1–2, 3.2). He argues that arrangements like those he describes in Persia and Sparta ensure that boys and young men develop appropriate self-discipline and good habits. In Sparta, the education of boys is overseen by state-appointed tutors, and continues up to adulthood, a point at which discipline and exercise are particularly important (*LP* 3.1–2). In both Sparta and Persia, Xenophon identifies competition between the young for honour as a driver of moral as well as physical excellence.

Xenophon is concerned in the opening sections of the *Memorabilia* to defend Socrates as an educator, since his teaching drove one of the charges against him, that he corrupted the young (*Mem.* 1.2.1), an assessment that Xenophon finds 'astonishing' and attempts to rebut in detail. Xenophon knows that this charge rested on the fact that several of Socrates' associates had betrayed the city or participated in the 404–403 oligarchy, and that his prosecutors blamed Socrates for the actions of Critias, Alcibiades, and others. But Xenophon argues that these men sought out Socrates for the advantages which studying with him would give them – the increased ability to argue, for example – and that they did not experience the real, moral benefits of his teaching (1.2.24–5). Socrates was banned from teaching, indeed from speaking to young people at all, by the Thirty (1.2.38–41).

Xenophon also places Socrates in his intellectual context, marking out his difference from natural philosophers such as Anaxagoras with their worryingly unconventional religious views. He first asserts Socrates' religious conventionality, showing how he conforms to correct practice both in his regular actions and also in encouraging others to honour the gods through offerings (*Mem.* 1.3.1–4). In Socrates' subsequent conversation with Aristodemus, who holds unconventional views and does not sacrifice to the usual gods, he sets out reasons for adhering to conventional practice, and gives an account of the power of the traditional gods expressed in terms which accommodate the newer discourse (1.4.2).

Xenophon shows Socrates carefully rebutting Aristodemus' views with an argument from the conscious design of the universe by a divine creator.[5] He points to natural desires – such as those of humans to procreate, of mothers to raise their children, and of children to live – as proof of a divine element in the workings of nature, and goes on to describe the omnipresence of the divine mind even where it cannot be perceived (1.4.7). Aristodemus counters with a common argument, that the gods have no concern for humans (1.4.11), but again Socrates responds with an argument based on the physical design of human beings as evidence that they are part of a cosmos created by an intelligent designer.

Through these two chapters, Xenophon makes it clear that the religious accusation against Socrates was groundless. However, he does also have to account for Socrates' religious peculiarity: his unusual communications from the gods voiced by his *daimonion* (*Mem.* 1.3.5; *Apol.* 8, 12–13). His depiction of the uproar at Socrates' trial acknowledges the jurors' objection to the idea that Socrates receives direct information and so has greater favour with the gods than they do.

In *Memorabilia* 4, Xenophon gives an idealized account of the teaching and encouragement which Socrates did provide, describing his attempt to educate Euthydemus, a young Athenian whom he meets in a saddler's shop at the edge of the *agora*, where the youth, too young to go into the marketplace to conduct business as an adult would, is sitting (*Mem.* 4.2.1).[6] As Christopher Moore has shown, this chapter offers an education in developing self-knowledge, in accordance with the Socratic Delphic maxim.[7] Euthydemus is eager to learn but clueless about how to do so; he has bought many books, but lacks the

---

[5] Dillery 1995: 186–94; Sedley 2007: 78–86.
[6] Johnson 2005a.
[7] Moore 2015: 216–35.

experience and knowledge to make any sense of them. Socrates engages him in conversation to expose the limits of his knowledge; Euthydemus' conventional ideas about justice fall apart under Socratic challenge. Socrates does not dispute Euthydemus' assertion that one cannot be a good citizen without being just (4.2.11), but under his probing Euthydemus is unable to determine what actions can be counted as just or not. The unjust acts which Euthydemus lists might be just in certain circumstances when deployed against enemies and performed to produce good ends: telling a lie is an unjust act, but a military commander might use deception to wrongfoot the enemy. And while Euthydemus readily concedes that deceiving enemies is just, Socrates suggests that deceiving your own citizens or troops might also be just if it improves morale and enables them to act (4.2.15–17).

The followers of Leo Strauss have extrapolated from Strauss's point that Euthydemus 'has a poor nature' the thought that Xenophon here represents the opposite of a Socratic education of a promising student.[8] However, there is no textual basis for this view; Euthydemus is gauche and ill-informed, but not irredeemable or ineducable. His inability to learn from books echoes Plato's views on the limits of writing as a means of transferring and inculcating knowledge. Socrates gently corrects Euthydemus' naïve rejection of religious custom and encourages him to follow 'the customary practice of his city' (4.3.16–18); Xenophon uses the youth to show how Socrates improved his students as participants in civic religion. The programme set out in *Memorabilia* 4 also makes clear the centrality of justice in interpersonal relations mediated through civic structures (4.4).

A key chapter (*Mem.* 4.5) establishes the personal values which the good citizen should demonstrate, particularly self-control (*enkrateia*) and moderation (*sōphrosunē*). Xenophon describes the citizen who has gained mastery of himself in opposition to the enslaved individual, who is imagined as lacking any capacity of self-management. Exercising freedom is impossible if one lacks self-control; such a condition is 'the worst form of slavery' (4.5.5) and akin to being an animal, not a human (4.5.11). Full control over physical appetites creates the space within which useful activity such as civic participation becomes possible (4.5.9–10). While this discussion sets out the

---

[8] L. Strauss 1972: 94; Pangle 2018: 166–7.

importance of self-mastery as a prelude to action, it does so at the cost of dehumanizing the enslaved who form the counter-example to the citizen who has achieved self-mastery.

Some have thought that Xenophon's depiction of Socrates' educational method is deficient, because he makes little use of the elenchus, a method in which questions and answers lead to a definition or failure. When he does depict an elenchus, it is often abbreviated and the argument incomplete.[9] While the detailed rules for this mode of argument are a *post hoc* rationalization by modern scholars, nonetheless Xenophon presents the elenchus as an initial form of discussion, intended to dispel misplaced self-confidence. Once a student has acknowledged their ignorance, Socrates moves on in established teacher–student relationships to giving speeches of encouragement and advice, intended to move students into self-improvement (*Mem.* 4.2.40).[10]

The contest for custom between different educators, often described as 'sophists', motivates significant parts of fourth-century Athenian prose. The term *sophistēs* developed in meaning over the course of Xenophon's life, and a tension between earlier and later senses, and the educators to whom they were applied, is clearly evident in Plato's Socratic dialogues. Plato criticizes a range of other educators, while Isocrates neatly sets out the rival groups in his abbreviated *Against the Sophists*. Xenophon is not a professional educator and not directly involved in this dispute, but he alludes to it in a diatribe on education which sits oddly within the practical advice on hunting in the *Cynegeticus*.[11]

In this passage, Xenophon distinguishes the sophists of the present from 'lovers of wisdom' (*Cyn.* 13.6), and sharply criticizes the way in which these sophists teach linguistic trickery rather than anything beneficial to the individual or the community (*Cyn.* 13.1–3). This is similar to the points that others make against eristic philosophers, and to criticisms of earlier teachers. Xenophon argues that practising hunting is a better training in commitment to communal values, because it is a collective enterprise which relies on shared resources.

---

[9] On Plato's depiction of the elenchus, see Vlastos 1994: 1–37; Benson 2010. On Xenophon's depictions, see Danzig 2017; Lachance 2018.

[10] On whether there is a genre of philosophical 'protreptic' to which this dialogue belongs, see Collins 2015: 16–34.

[11] Some have assumed that this section is an interpolation: see L'Allier 2008.

This point is even more true in Sparta, where sharing hunting dogs and other equipment was customary (*LP* 6.3). The same point is expanded in the *Cyropaedia*, where Cyrus' father, Cambyses, notes that a teacher visiting Persia in the past brought Greek-style teaching, in which boys studied both telling the truth and lying, in order to win arguments against each other (1.6.31–2). These boys did not stop seeking unfair advantage in their dealings with others, and as a result such teaching was made illegal in the hope of developing 'more gentle citizens' (1.6.33). This seems a direct if anachronistic critique of elements of the sophistic education of Athens, such as the use of 'double arguments' for and against a position.[12]

Modelling the ideal city

Xenophon saw education as preparation for political participation and leadership in cities whose systems of rule and cultural practices he examined in his writings, sometimes using the *politeia* form to explore political ideas. We have one standalone *politeia* text by him, the *Constitution of the Spartans*, and one embedded within a fictional narrative, that of Persia (*Cyropaedia* 1.2); in both cases, he describes a *politeia* established in the past, which present citizens fail to adhere to.[13] Some other contemporary *politeia* texts took a critical perspective and did not aim at comprehensive coverage of their subjects, an approach exemplified by the *Constitution of the Athenians* long attributed to Xenophon, which criticizes Athenian democracy but makes careful note of its successful features.

Xenophon values political stability, which he regards as best achieved by adherence to long-standing laws; in Sparta, the laws of Lycurgus met this criterion. He places the establishment of the Lycurgan *politeia* much earlier than other ancient sources do, at the time of the Heraclids, the Peloponnesians who returned to Sparta following the end of the Trojan War (*LP* 10.8).[14] Like Herodotus, Xenophon notes the involvement of the oracle at Delphi in the establishment of the

---

[12] See Bonazzi 2020: 1–10.

[13] Bordes 1982: 70–1, 176–203; see also Atack 2018c.

[14] Humble 2022: 49; this would place Lycurgus in the very distant past, while others position him in the more historical eighth century BCE. See Plut. *Vit. Lyc.* 1; Hdt. 1.65.2–66.1; Pl. *Leg.* 3.691d–692c.

politeia (*LP* 8.5; Hdt. 1.65–6); this makes obeying the laws a religious as well as a political obligation.

However, Xenophon's focus is not on political institutions, but on the social institutions which structure the daily lives of Sparta's citizen elite, including the communal meals, the sharing of property, and interpersonal relationships within and beyond the family, especially the rearing of children and training of youths. Unlike in other cities, economic activity is forbidden to the elite citizen class (7.1–3), and there is no precious-metal currency through which private wealth can be hoarded (7.5–6). Xenophon emphasizes the centrality to Sparta's political culture of obedience (*to peithesthai*) to the laws, and the increasing importance of the ephors, annually elected officials who monitored political obedience and had summary powers of punishment (8.1–4).

Persia's laws and customs, as set out in the *Cyropaedia*, are presented as long-established; although Xenophon does not give a foundation story for them, he frequently notes their persistence. His model Persia is a community in which the effort of the elite to embody virtue is properly rewarded. Many commentators treat it as a republic with a mixed constitution, in which the leading citizens largely administer themselves according to prescribed norms under the oversight of a constitutional monarch, equally restrained by convention.[15] However, there are limitations to individual freedom and choice; Cambyses, Cyrus' father, is able to mandate participation in hunting expeditions (*Cyr.* 1.2.10). The Persians are acculturated to their laws through their state-managed education, and so have no thought of transgressing them (1.2.3, 15), suggesting that this republic exemplifies 'positive' rather than 'negative' freedom, in Isaiah Berlin's terminology.[16]

Like many *politeiai*, Xenophon's account describes the physical space of the city as a way of exploring its social structure and hierarchy. He separates virtuous civic leadership from business by locating civic activity and trade in separate spaces: a 'free town square' (*eleuthera agora*) by the royal palace and administrative offices; and a separate space for business. The layout of the civic *agora* itself is arranged to provide space for each age class, for the separate activities of boys, youths, men of age to provide military service, and elders (*Cyr.* 1.2.4). Xenophon goes into a great deal of detail in describing the

---

[15] For 'Republican' readings of Xenophon's Persia, see Newell 1983; Nadon 1996.
[16] Berlin 1969.

hunting expeditions which form part of the training of the young, and the discipline imposed on participants, who are encouraged not to eat while engaged in hunting (1.2.11). He also lists the different military skills deployed by different age groups, as they progress from youths using distance weapons such as bow and arrow to adult men training with close combat weapons. But he then turns to the role of the elders: once men are too old for military service, they play a greater role in administering justice, conducting trials which can result in wrongdoers being disenfranchised and disgraced (1.2.14). Although Persia is populous, only a small proportion enters the first, educational stage, of this *cursus honorum*, and even fewer reach the final stage.

Cyrus later describes a key aspect of Persian education: its focus on justice. Boys prosecute and defend each other in mock trials, and are also punished by their teachers (1.2.6–7). Cyrus himself is punished when he intervenes in a dispute between two boys about the ownership of a cloak (1.3.16–17).[17] He has attempted to redistribute the cloaks, so that each boy has the one which fits him best rather than the one which belongs to him, but this contravenes the accepted sense of justice, and so, he explains to his mother, Mandane, the beating he received has taught him about Persian justice.

While the Persians think that this set of practices will make their citizens 'the best' (1.2.15), Xenophon does not consider here the consequences for those who do not manage to progress or participate in this process. Yet he recounts the consequences in Sparta of excluding from governance and civic honour those who failed to meet the wealth classification required to belong to the Spartiate elite, and the possibility that they might ally with other lower classes. Downward mobility caused the disaffection at Sparta which led to the Cinadon conspiracy and revolt early in the reign of Agesilaus, suggesting the precarity of his grasp on power (*Hell.* 3.3.4–11).[18]

Spartan kings might promote the interests of their friends, as Agesilaus did in protecting Sphodrias from punishment after his disastrous failed attempt to capture the Piraeus in 378 (*Hell.* 5.4.19–24). He was acquitted after an intervention by the king, motivated partly by the fact that their sons Archidamus and Cleonymus were lovers (5.4.25–33), resulting in what many thought to be the 'most unjust' (*adikōtata*) verdict ever delivered in a Spartan court.

---

[17] Danzig 2009. For more on this scene in its monarchical context, see Chapter 6.
[18] Cartledge 2002: 67–9, 234–5; Gish 2009.

Xenophon structures his narrative so that the young Cleonymus' dedi-
cation to his country, and his heroic death at the battle of Leuctra in
371, become the conclusion. This framing presents his narrative as
an exemplary one, despite the critical elements.

Some of Xenophon's contemporaries, notably Isocrates, valorized a
past version of Athens as an ideal. Xenophon presents Athenian
politicians, notably the moderate oligarch Theramenes, engaging in
this discourse and appealing to the city's long-established laws and
customs to justify political resistance (see pp. 72–3). He also has
Socrates suggest, in a conversation with the aspiring general Pericles
junior, that the Athens of the present has declined in culture as well
as in its empire and influence:

'My own view', Socrates replied, 'is that rather as it can happen with athletes who have
been far ahead of the field and won everything – they can relax their efforts and fall
behind the competition – in the same way the Athenians, after all that clear superiority,
have neglected (*amelēsas*) themselves and so fallen into decline.'
   'So what now can they do to recover their old quality (*archaian aretēn*)?'
   'There's no mystery, it seems to me,' said Socrates. 'If they rediscover the practices
followed by their ancestors *(ta tōn progonōn epitedeumata)* and follow them as well as
they did, they would become just as good as their ancestors.'

                                                                              (*Mem.* 3.5.13–14)

These deeds featured in the rhetoric of the Athenian funeral speech,
and so point to Pericles senior's omission of such patriotic elements
in the speech given to him by Thucydides.[19]

Athens thus fits into a model which applies to Sparta and Persia as
well: an ideal past version of the city achieved success, including the
establishment of a good *politeia* and cultural norms, but the present-day
citizens do not live up to those values. Xenophon expresses this
explicitly for Sparta and Persia in two chapters which have been
considered interpolations to his work (*LP* 14; *Cyr.* 8.8), but which
make an argument consistent with the *Memorabilia* passage and other
'ancestral constitution' arguments of his time regarding the problem
of cultural decline.[20] The present-day Spartans have lost sight of their
traditional values, seeking to gain riches, including making money
from holding office overseas (*LP* 14.3–5). As he has previously identified the Lycurgan *politeia* as sanctioned by a divine law, because of its

---

[19] Thuc. 2.35–46. See also Lysias 2; Loraux 1986; McNamara 2009.
[20] See Humble 2004, 2022: 52–61, 188–97.

authorization by Delphi, this disregard for the city's political and cultural norms is an act of impiety (14.6).

A similar situation holds in Persia, although here Xenophon describes a decline after Cyrus' death, when the Persian elite cease to uphold their traditional values and have become unprincipled and unjust, as seen in their dishonesty (*Cyr.* 8.8.6), drunkenness (8.8.10), unwillingness to exercise (8.8.8, 12), and neglect of traditional education (8.8.13–14). While Xenophon's authorship of this description of moral collapse has been doubted by some, and others have taken it to reveal a hidden criticism of Cyrus himself, Vivienne Gray has shown how its careful structure reflects critiques of political decline in Sparta and Athens.[21] Elsewhere, Xenophon has Socrates praise the stability of the Lycurgan laws, and argue that a lack of change makes *homonoia*, agreement among the citizens, more likely: 'Because the cities whose people abide by the laws prove the strongest and the most prosperous (*eudaimonestatoi*). Without unanimity (*homonoia*) there can be no good government of a city or good management of a household' (*Mem.* 4.4.16). Socrates contrasts the stability of Spartan law with the situation at Athens, where, as his interlocutor Hippias has observed, laws are easily changed; citizens can introduce proposals in the assembly which may be enacted as decrees with legal force (*Mem.* 4.4.14).

Xenophon's comparative thought on constitutions runs deeper than a *post hoc* justification of his preference for Spartan traditions over Athenian practice. It would be possible for a democracy to operate with respect for its original traditions, and for change to be less easy to bring about than he suggests that it is. His account of civil conflict in Athens (*Hell.* 2.2–4) and his suggestions for improving the city's finances (*Poroi*) suggest that his respect for established tradition did not preclude experiment in response to changing circumstances. Despite his love of tradition, he was not simply an originalist.

The Socratic citizen: elite participation in democracy

Xenophon's writing on the city has two main focuses. One is the way in which a citizen – implicitly a member of the moneyed elite – can participate in civic life, and indeed may be obligated to do so, according

---

[21] Miller 1914: 438–9 brackets the whole chapter. See also Gera 1993: 299–300; Nadon 2001: 139–46; Dorion 2010; Gray 2011b: 246–63.

to the Socratic value system. A second, more practical concern considers the risks and rewards inherent in so doing. This section sets out Xenophon's model of ethical engagement with public life, much of it voiced by Socrates in the *Memorabilia* and so contributing towards Xenophon's defence of Socrates as a teacher of elite citizens. Xenophon attempts to explain to young men of elite status why they should participate in the political life of the city, and accept commanding roles in the military, even though these roles may place them at risk of trial and punishments, including exile and death. Although Socrates' punishment and his own exile might motivate this concern, Xenophon associates the theme with wider political debates, from the connection between political power and the search for pleasure, to the role of civic participation in self-realization. Although, like Plato, he sets his discussion in the lifetime of Socrates, the hedonism of Aristippus and the Cyrenaics was a challenge for philosophers of his own time, leading him to argue that the ethical life was one of political and community involvement.

In his *Oeconomicus*, Xenophon emphasizes the importance of good management and oversight in a domestic context, but the key activity of *epimeleia* is also that of the citizen and leader in the context of the *polis* and its institutions. Managing and administering are activities through which personal virtues can be activated. In this sense, taking part in civic life in a leadership role is necessary for a Xenophontic good citizen to demonstrate and actualize the capacities developed through a Socratic education. There may be some irony in Xenophon's own enforced absence from civic life as an exile.

The question of political involvement is most closely scrutinized in Socrates' dialogue with the fictionalized young Aristippus, a hedonist who disclaims loyalty to any *polis*. Here, Xenophon sets out a case for political obligation, underscored by the story of the young Heracles at the Crossroads and his choice between Virtue and Vice (*Mem.* 2.1.21–34).[22] While the fable has often been read on its own, it should be seen as a counter to the arguments expressed by Aristippus in the first half of the dialogue, and as a strong claim that, as Thomas Pangle notes, 'the transpolitical, philosophic life should and could never leave behind civic engagement'.[23] Notably, Xenophon creates the model of the engaged citizen in opposition to the figure of the slave, explicitly identifying Aristippus as a slave-owner (2.1.5).

---

[22] On links between Aristippus and the Socratics, see Tsouna-McKirahan 1994; Tsouna 2020.
[23] Pangle 2018: 63. See also L. Strauss 1972: 32–9; Sansone 2004; Johnson 2009.

Aristippus outlines the risks of political participation – prosecution and misery – invoking the analogy of enslavement in a paradoxical inversion where it is the rulers who are enslaved to the ordinary citizens:

Cities expect to treat their rulers as I do my household slaves. I expect my servants to provide me with a limitless supply of the necessaries, but not to touch any of them themselves, and cities likewise think that their rulers should bring them maximum benefit while keeping their own hands off any part of it. So I would class as potential rulers those who want to have a lot of trouble themselves and cause a lot of trouble to others, and I would have them educated as you suggest: but as for me personally, I class myself among those who want to lead as easy and enjoyable life as they can.

(Mem. 2.1.9)

What Aristippus seeks to avoid is either of the states that a citizen in a democracy might occupy: that of ruling or that of being ruled (2.1.11); he argues that there is a middle way 'of freedom', which will spare him from the apparent servitude involved in both the other roles.

Socrates disputes that this is the case, using examples which point to the invasion of Attica by the Spartans during the Peloponnesian War. There is no way to opt out of the conflict of civil life:

Or are you unaware of the people who cut the grain and fell the trees that others have sown and planted, and use every means of starving out the weaker folk who refuse them subservience, until they prevail on them to opt for slavery rather than a fight against the stronger?   (Mem. 2.1.13)

Aristippus claims in response that he can enjoy guest status without incurring social obligation or needing to defer to other community members. To Socrates, this is an idle fantasy. But for Aristippus, the kind of voluntary sacrifice of effort which Socrates commends for the elite is foolish:

But given that, Socrates, what about those who are being educated for 'the royal art of government' (basilikē technē), which you seem to equate with happiness (eudaimonia)? How do they differ from people compelled to hardship, if they must willingly submit to hunger, thirst, cold, sleeplessness, and all those other tribulations? For my part I can't see any difference between a voluntary and an involuntary flogging – it's the same skin – or generally between submitting willingly or unwillingly to all such assaults on one's body: again, it's the same body. The only difference, is it not, is the added folly of the man who volunteers to endure the suffering?   (Mem. 2.1.17)

Xenophon here skirmishes with sophistic arguments about power and pleasure; Aristippus echoes the views of such Platonic characters as Thrasymachus (Republic 1) and Polus (Gorgias), for whom power implies the unrestricted capacity to pursue individual pleasure.[24] He also suggests that the paradoxes expressed by Plato's Socrates are not an obvious answer to these arguments, and offers an alternative way of countering them, through the above-mentioned fable of Heracles at the Crossroads, which he attributes to the sophist Prodicus of Ceos, although its language is particularly Xenophontic.[25]

In the story, the young Heracles encounters two mysterious women who turn out to be personifications of Virtue and Vice, and who set out the attractions of their different approaches to life (2.1.22). Their physical embodiment matches the distinction drawn in the *Oeconomicus* between the good and bad performance of womanhood: Virtue is modest in dress and demeanour, whereas Vice flaunts her abundant flesh through revealing clothes.[26]

After Xenophon has considered the personal relationships of male citizens in Book 2 of the *Memorabilia*, he returns in Book 3 to the question of their engagement in political life. Other elite citizens may try to avoid the attention brought by a public career, to manage their affairs as privately as possible in the context of the city.[27] One character who has succeeded in this quietist approach is Charmides (*Mem.* 3.7), whom Socrates persuades to use his management skills for public benefit, just as he has done in his private life. Xenophon must be deploying a form of irony here, as the historical Charmides, Plato's uncle, held a significant office under the Thirty as one of the board of Ten overseeing the Piraeus, before being killed in the civil war.[28] Nonetheless, it is to Charmides that Socrates asserts most explicitly the importance of involvement in civic life: 'Good government will be a benefit not only to the other citizens, but also to your friends and, not least, to you yourself' (*Mem.* 3.7.9).

Some of Socrates' other interlocutors have suffered from the enmity of their fellow citizens. A public reputation for wealth attracted negative attention from vexatious litigants and other hangers-on, who saw that they could easily make money if their target settled rather than go to court. This is a problem faced by his friend Crito (*Mem.* 2.9.1).[29] Socrates finds a practical solution for him: he employs the impoverished

---

[24] Lampe 2015.
[25] Gray 2006.
[26] Glazebrook 2009, Murnaghan 1988.
[27] Carter 1986; Christ 2006.
[28] Nails 2002: 90–4.
[29] Mirroring Plato's *Crito*, in which Crito advises Socrates on his legal situation.

but talented Archedemus to see off court cases and protect his interests (*Mem.* 2.9.4–8).

Xenophon also takes a critical look at Spartan political culture and the exclusion of the majority from active participation in political life. While his account of the Spartan constitution began with praise of Lycurgus, its penultimate chapter criticizes present-day Spartans for their failure to maintain the virtuous habits inculcated by Lycurgus' *politeia*. Xenophon is aware of the class conflict that has developed, as members of elite families have slipped out of the highest property classification and the right to full political participation. This is the background to the conspiracy of Cinadon early in Agesilaus' reign (*Hell.* 3.3.4–11). The young ex-Spartiate sought the equal status denied to him through impoverishment, hoping to engage broad support from the classes below the Spartiate elite, but probably not succeeding in doing so before being reported to the ephors. As Cawkwell notes, Xenophon's account gives us insights into Spartan social structures not available elsewhere.[30]

Just as Xenophon depicted the free flow of information through Athens (p. 69), he shows the way it was controlled in Sparta. When news of the defeat at Leuctra arrived during the celebration of the festival of the Gymnopaidiai, the choral performance continues. The ephors inform the families of men who died, but tell them not to wail or lament; the following day, the bereaved appear proud in public, while the families of survivors display their shame (*Hell.* 6.4.16).

The city and democracy

No work of Xenophon's provides a single theorized consideration of Athenian democracy, or of democracy more generally.[31] But although he used other locations for much of his work, Athens remained central to his thought as, in Matthew Christ's analysis, an engaged critic of the city's democratic regime.[32] Xenophon's ambiguous criticism of both democracy and oligarchy is contained in his most detailed historical narrative (*Hell.* 1–2), which covers the end of the Peloponnesian War, the rule of the Thirty in 404/3 BCE, and the civil war which restored

[30] Cawkwell 1979: 161; Gish 2009.
[31] Dillery 1995: 146–63; on Xenophon's work as political thought, see Gray 2007.
[32] Christ 2020: 26–31.

the democracy, and it offers, in John Dillery's words, 'a prospective paradigm of the bad community that fails'.[33]

Rather than a complete linear narrative, Xenophon provides a series of exemplary portraits of the leaders who represent different responses to the civic struggle, and a typology of political attitudes, comparable with Plato's more abstract descriptions of the personalities related to regime types (*Republic* Books 8–9). Greek political thinking often features analogies, such as that between the individual soul and the city (Pl. *Rep.* 2.368e–369a, 4.435de), and that between the individual body and the corporate political entity (Arist. *Pol.* 3.11.1281a39–b15).[34] The *polis* was, after all, nothing more, nor less, than its collected citizens.

Xenophon thus imposes a pattern on his narrative as he moves from the fragile democracy in the closing stages of the Peloponnesian War to the advent of the Thirty and the descent into civil war, an account which contains some of his sharpest political commentary and most vivid descriptions. It starts with the final stages of the Peloponnesian War, at a point when Athens' defeat was becoming inevitable. Thucydides' narrative breaks off in 411, at a point when Athens appears to be recovering from the massive blow of the loss of the Sicilian Expedition, and is beginning to re-establish its democracy (Thuc. 8.98.4, 106.1).[35] Xenophon claims to begin 'not many days later' than events narrated by Thucydides (*Hell.* 1.1.1), although there is a gap. But, like Thucydides, Xenophon arranges his narrative around the acts of specific commanders, in this case Alcibiades, welcomed back to Athens in 407 and now fighting for his city in the eastern Aegean. His initial successes are followed by defeat by the Spartans under Lysander at Notium (*Hell.* 1.5.16). In one of the first instances of a repeating pattern in the *Hellenica*, Athens votes to relieve Alcibiades of his command; Hermocrates of Syracuse, a general praised by Thucydides for his outstanding intelligence (Thuc. 6.72.2), is also exiled by his city while in the field, to the dismay of his troops (*Hell.* 1.1.27–31, 1.3.13).

Arginusae

A key episode is the account of the trial in 406/5 BCE of the Arginusae generals (*Hell.* 1.7).[36] This is not a dispassionate or unbiased account of

[33] Dillery 1995: 147.
[34] Brock 2013: 69–82; see also Brock 2004.
[35] Dillery 1995: 9–11; Rood 2004c.
[36] See Andrewes 1974; Due 1983; Pownall 2000; Christ 2020: 17–26.

democratic procedure, but an exemplary account of an attempt to uphold the law in the face of the manipulation of the masses by populist factions among the elite. It features several characters developed elsewhere in Xenophon's work: Socrates, the younger Pericles (*Mem.* 3.5), and Thrasybulus and Theramenes, who go on to be significant players in the civil war.

The story begins with a fraught naval battle in the waters around the Arginusae islands, between Lesbos and the Lydian coast. During the battle twenty-five Athenian ships are lost, and the Athenians are unable to collect the bodies of the dead or rescue the shipwrecked, because, as Xenophon emphasizes, a storm blows up (*Hell.* 1.6.29–34, 1.7.29–31). Xenophon's main interest is to reveal the illegality and unfairness of the subsequent prosecution at Athens, and the manipulation of democratic processes which lead to the generals' conviction. He sets out the complex and multi-stage processes which characterized Athenian politics and justice: a procedural attack on two of the generals, on an unrelated charge of fraudulent handling of public funds, is replaced by a single prosecution against them all – illegal under Athenian legal convention (1.7.2–5). Although the assembly eagerly take up this proposal, it runs out of time as, after a long day, it becomes too dark to take a vote, and the motion to condemn the generals is postponed to another assembly meeting.

Xenophon shows pressure to prosecute the generals becoming a factional matter as the populist Theramenes, who was the naval officer charged with retrieving the dead, attempts to strengthen feeling against his commanders, by paying for people to appear as mourners bereaved by the incident at the Apaturia, a key Athenian festival at which sons honoured their fathers and new citizens were enrolled (*Hell.* 1.7.8).[37] Theramenes also bribes Callixeinos, a member of the Council, to attack the generals, and he goes on to propose the motion condemning them.

Xenophon's narrative of the assembly meeting which serves as a trial focuses on one man, Euryptolemus, a relative of the younger Pericles, one of those charged, and a cousin and aide-de-camp to Alcibiades.[38] He sets out the popular response:

Some of the people praised this, but the masses (*plēthos*) cried that it was terrible if anyone prevented the people (*dēmos*) from doing whatever it wanted. On top of this,

---

[37] R. Parker 2007: 458–61.
[38] *Hell.* 1.4.19. See Gray 1989: 83–91; Nails 2002: 150.

when Lyciscus proposed that these men should be tried with the same vote as the generals, unless they withdrew this summons, the crowd (*ochlos*) erupted in disorder again, and they were forced to give up on it.   (*Hell.* 1.7.12–13)

Frances Pownall noted the shift in language here, as Xenophon deploys pejorative terms to show his disapproval of the actions of the people.[39] Launching a counter-suit that a proposal was 'contrary to the law' (a type of case known as a *graphē paranomōn*), by suing its originator, was becoming an important manoeuvre in the Athenian assembly and courts.[40]

Xenophon links this episode to his defence of Socrates, who, he says, was the chair of the assembly meeting in question (1.7.15), a duty which might fall by lot to any citizen who had been selected as a member of the Council (*boulē*) during the month when their tribe held the presidency.[41] Socrates 'said that he would not do anything contrary to the law'. In the *Memorabilia*, Xenophon adds that Socrates 'thought it more important to abide by his oath than to give in to an illegal popular demand or protect himself against intimidation' (*Mem.* 1.1.18). However, the other presiding councillors took the easier option of accepting the motion onto the agenda, and so it was debated and put to the vote.

As the trial continues, Euryptolemus speaks in defence of the generals as a group, taking in the role of justice and knowledge within the city (*Hell.* 1.7.16–33):

No! If you listen to me and take just and pious actions, by doing so you will best discover the truth and will not find out, after coming to realize it late, that you have committed the greatest crimes against both the gods and yourselves.

(*Hell.* 1.7.19)

For Xenophon, acting justly will generate political knowledge.[42]

The rhetorical conclusion of Euryptolemus' speech is a plea for the virtues of following due process:

---

[39] Pownall 2000: 500.

[40] Hansen 1999: 205–12.

[41] Rhodes 1972: 16–30; Hansen 1999: 250; and Cammack 2021 on active and passive roles in Athenian decision-making bodies.

[42] Xenophon's account of events is contradicted by the other ancient source for the episode, Diodorus Siculus 13.101, who emphasizes the personal dispute between the generals and the commanders Thrasybulus and Theramenes; see Andrewes 1974.

If these things are done, those who commit crimes will meet with the most severe punishment, while those who are blameless will be set free by you, men of Athens, and will not be wrongly killed. And you, respecting your religion and your oaths, will judge in accordance with the law, and not fight alongside the Spartans by putting to death without a trial and against the law those men who captured seventy of their ships and were victorious over them.   (*Hell.* 1.7.24–5)

Xenophon's alignment of piety and observance of the law, as well as his practical concern for the maintenance of military resources, are evident throughout the speech, which provides a frame for reading his account of generals and their actions in subsequent conflicts.[43]

The end of the war and the advent of the Thirty

The Athenian politicians Theramenes and Thrasybulus emerge as significant actors as opponents of the post-war oligarchic regime of 404/3. Xenophon's narrative follows Theramenes' change of heart with sympathy and agreement, suggesting that the author followed a similar trajectory of disillusionment.[44]

Successive defeats at sea, particularly that at Aegospotami in the Hellespont in 405, pointed to an inevitable defeat for a city which was still, as Xenophon depicts it, capable of decisive collective action. He provides a vivid description of the arrival of the news of defeat on the city's messenger trireme, the *Paralus*, and artfully frames the frantic response to the Spartans' anticipated actions:

When the Paralus arrived at Athens in the night, they began to speak about the disaster. The wailing passed from the Piraeus through the Long Walls up to the city, one man announcing the news to another, and nobody slept that night, not just mourning the dead, but even more mourning themselves, thinking that they too would suffer what they had done to the Melians, as Spartan colonists, defeating them through a siege, and the Histiaeans and the Scionaeans and the Toronaeans and the Aeginetans and many other Greeks. On the next day they held an assembly, in which they decided to block all their harbours but one, to put the walls in good order, to position guards, and to get ready for a siege in every other respect. And that is what they did.   (*Hell.* 2.2.3–4)

Xenophon echoes Thucydides' report of the arrival of the news of the loss of the Sicilian Expedition, barely a decade previously, which had eventually triggered a brief replacement of the democracy by

---

[43] Tuplin 1993.
[44] See Chapter 2.

oligarchy.[45] His account shows the movement of information from the harbour to the heart of the city, but, although the information spreads in a disorderly way as a rumour, the response of the city's democratic institutions is swift and decisive, and does not betray the political fault-lines which will shortly emerge.

The defeat at Aegospotami closed off vital grain supplies from the Black Sea, which enabled the Spartan commander Lysander to starve the city out from a distance (2.2.10–11). Athens attempted to negotiate; after an initial round of talks failed, Theramenes asked to be sent to discuss possible terms for peace with Lysander (2.2.16–20).[46] After several months, possibly delaying Athens' surrender, he returned to the city with a harsh offer which would demilitarize the city, although Xenophon suggests that it was Sparta's allies Corinth and Thebes, rather than Sparta itself, who insisted on this (2.2.19). Athens was required to demolish the Long Walls which connected the city to its harbour at the Piraeus, and the fortifications there, as well as committing to acting in support of Sparta. Xenophon reports the return of the embassy and the Athenian response:

Theramenes and the ambassadors who were with him brought these terms back to Athens. A great crowd (*ochlos*) surrounded them as they entered the city, fearing that they had come back without completing their task. For there was no longer any time to delay, on account of the number (*plēthos*) of people dying from hunger. On the next day the ambassadors reported the conditions under which the Spartans would make peace; Theramenes argued for the deal, saying that it was necessary to obey the Spartans and take down the walls. Some people spoke against this, but a much greater number joined in agreeing to them, and it was decided to accept the peace terms. After this Lysander sailed into the Piraeus, the exiles returned, and, thinking that this day was the beginning of freedom (*eleutherias*) for Greece, they eagerly tore down the walls as flute-girls played.   (*Hell.* 2.2.22–4)

Again, although more briefly, the dockside scene becomes a place for the display of public mood, and the assembly one of unresolved conflict, in contrast to the decisive action after Aegospotami. Xenophon's quick sketch provides more than a vivid image; the sympotic performance of the destruction of the walls suggests the pro-Spartan enthusiasm of Athens' conservative elite.[47] This may hint at the unrest to come.

---

[45] Thuc. 8.1.1; Rood 2012a: 78–80.
[46] Krentz 1982: 34–7; Dillery 1995: 23; Christ 2020: 32.
[47] Azoulay and Ismard 2020: 63.

Xenophon shows how the subsequent behaviour of the Thirty, the oligarchic regime installed by Sparta, rendered any optimism misplaced. Rather than solving the difficulties of Athenian democracy, the new regime quickly developed into a violent and destructive tyranny. Xenophon's own authorial stance shifts: he moves to showing the democratic resistance to the Thirty, and presenting the leaders of that resistance in a positive light, suggesting that his political preferences were not purely oligarchic. Scholars have not agreed on this shift: William Higgins detected a continuing sympathy for Critias, the leader of the regime, whereas Matthew Christ found Xenophon more critical of the Thirty.[48]

Xenophon reports the assembly decision to appoint a council of Thirty, who were supposed to 'write up the ancestral laws (*patrious nomous*)' (2.3.2). For Athenians the 'ancestral constitution' (*patrios politeia*) was largely a nostalgic fantasy, which had first emerged as a political programme during the previous oligarchic revolution in 411/ 10 ([Arist.] *Ath. Pol.* 29.3), and which remained a favoured project of Athenian conservatives throughout the fourth century, advocated by Isocrates and indeed by Xenophon in his visions of Sparta and Persia.[49] Although Xenophon notes Spartan involvement in the establishment of the Thirty, he represents the regime as chosen by the Athenians rather than imposed from outside; as John Dillery noted, his own experience under the regime may have affected his views, even if writing about the events decades later.[50]

Xenophon also shapes the story into a negative exemplum. He shows the new regime consolidating personal power and taking immediate action to appeal to its supporters.[51] The elite had long complained about harassment from vexatious prosecutions by other citizens bearing grudges (as happened to Crito, *Mem.* 2.9); now those in power could punish citizens who had used the courts to harass their political opponents (*Hell.* 2.3.12). There was little opposition to these figures being prosecuted and put to death. However, the new regime did not stop there, but sought Spartan military backing for a programme intended to eliminate political opposition (2.3.13).

---

[48] Higgins 1977: 108–9; Shear 2011: 180–7; Christ 2020: 26–7.
[49] See Fuks 1971; Rhodes 2006; Shear 2011: 167–75.
[50] Dillery 1995: 146–8.
[51] Xenophon does not explain that the peace settlement mandated the return to an 'ancestral constitution' ([Arist.] *Ath. Pol.* 34.3); see Rhodes 1993.

Opposition to the Thirty

Xenophon emphasizes the role of individuals in opposing the regime, starting with Theramenes, who argues that more citizens should be admitted to full participation in the regime:[52]

> But, while many were being killed, and unjustly so, many others were openly coming together in amazement at the state of the *politeia*, and Theramenes said again, that unless they admitted sufficient numbers into the administration as partners (*koinōnous*), it would be impossible for the oligarchy to continue.
>
> (*Hell.* 2.3.17)

However, the creation of a list of three thousand citizens (including Socrates) does not ameliorate the situation; rather than being empowered, these citizens are rounded up and their weapons removed, and Theramenes himself is arrested. Xenophon does not overlook the regime's violence.[53] The stage is set for a confrontation between Critias and Theramenes. Unusually, Xenophon presents a pair of speeches in which the opposed positions are clearly set out, Critias (2.3.24–34) voicing a hard-line *realpolitik* and Theramenes (2.3.35–49) a conservative but still democratic line.

Critias' opening words are particularly powerful:

> Gentlemen of the council, if any of you think that more men are being killed than the occasion demands (*kairou*), recall that whenever a regime is being changed anywhere this kind of thing happens. It is necessary that those setting up an oligarchy will have the most numerous enemies, because the city is the most populous of Greek states and because its people have been brought up in freedom for the longest time. But since we recognize that democracy is a difficult regime for people like you and us, and we also know that the people would never become friendly to the Spartans who saved us, but the best people (*beltistoi*) would always remain faithful, we set up this present regime with the approval of the Spartans. And if we perceive that someone is opposed to the oligarchy, we have him put out of the way, and most particularly, we think it right that if any of our own people is dissatisfied with this state of affairs (*katastasis*), he should be punished.   (*Hell.* 2.3.24–6)

Critias attempts to deflect criticism of the regime by attacking Theramenes' character; based on the way he appeared to have switched sides after Arginusae, Critias mocks him as a 'stage boot' (*cothurnos*, *Hell.* 2.3.31), after a shoe which could be worn on either foot.

---

[52] Krentz 1982: 67–8; Dillery 1995: 146–51.
[53] Dillery 1995: 146–63; Pownall 2019; Wolpert 2019.

Theramenes answers this and reasserts a moderate line, opposed to the extreme and equally changeable violence he attributes to Critias:

I am forever at war with those who think that there would be no good democracy until both slaves and those who would hand over the city for the lack of a drachma participate in politics, and indeed I am also opposed to those who think that there would be no good oligarchy until the city has been set up to be tyrannized by a few men. But I previously thought it best to benefit the government of the city with those who are capable, both with their shields and their horses, and I do not change that view now.

(*Hell.* 2.3.48)

This is the closest Xenophon comes to identifying his favoured form of democracy: full political participation for the section of citizens of sufficient means to serve as hoplites or in the cavalry.[54] This model, which might be seen as either a broad oligarchy or a narrow democracy, possibly resembles the so-called constitution of the 'Five Thousand' briefly in place in the earlier oligarchic revolution of 411/10, in which all those who could afford hoplite armour were granted full participation.[55] Aristotle, writing after Athenian democracy had been re-established, regards this form of democracy as earlier and less extreme (*Pol.* 4.4.1291b21–33); in this form of democracy, those with limited means for leisure need to restrict the amount of time they spend in the assembly and so accept the rule of law (*Pol.* 4.4.1291b30–38).

The final appearance of Theramenes continues the theme of political life as a sympotic performance which runs through this part of the *Hellenica*, and it confirms his elite status as an internal critic of the regime.[56] The condemned man demonstrates his contempt by toasting Critias with the hemlock he has been condemned to drink, and flinging the dregs from a cup as if he were playing the party game of *kottabos* (*Hell.* 2.3.56).

Law and justice

In his accounts of the Arginusae trial and of the democracy's treatment of subsequent generals, Xenophon insists on the centrality of law and justice to the existence of community. This matches the value placed

---

[54] Christ 2020: 30.

[55] Thucydides had described the Athenians as 'conducting political life well (*eu politeusantes*) for the first time in my experience', on the basis of a mixed regime (8.97.2).

[56] Azoulay and Ismard 2020: 70–1.

on law in the Spartan and Persian *politeiai*. In his more theoretical exploration of law in the *Memorabilia*, Xenophon regards it as a way of ensuring that social order reflects the cosmic order of the gods, including 'unwritten laws' (*Mem.* 4.4.19) that govern conventional morality.[57] He also shows Socrates instilling respect for the law in his associates.

While Xenophon is concerned with defending Socrates against both the actual charges brought against him and also the underlying suspicion that Socrates was responsible for the illegal acts of his former students (*Mem.* 1.2.12–39), he has a wider concern that democratic factionalism had led to the manipulation and misuse of the law, so that it no longer fulfils its function in maintaining cosmic order. He emphasizes the oaths sworn when the democratic party imposed peace terms after the brutal Athenian civil war of 404/3; Thrasybulus asks that his opponents show that they can keep their oaths and respect the gods (*euorkoi kai hosioi*), and observe the ancient laws (*nomois archaiois*, *Hell.* 2.4.42).

Socrates and Athens

In Xenophon's version of the Arginusae trial, Socrates stands as an exemplar of the ordinary citizen carrying out his political duty for the public good (*Hell.* 1.7.15). Xenophon's other depiction of an Athenian trial, that of Socrates in the court of the King Archon, is contained within his *Apology*. Here, Xenophon is explicit that he is not setting out a full account of the events, but trying to explain why Socrates' defence of his religious practice, centred on his belief that a *daimonion* or spirit offered him personal guidance which was of benefit to his fellow citizens, came across to the jurors as arrogant.[58] Xenophon concludes that 'by singing his own praises in court he invited the resentment of the jury and made them more inclined to convict him' (*Apol.* 32).

In the *Memorabilia*, Xenophon explores the likely underlying reason for prejudice against Socrates: his role in educating wealthy upper-class citizens, future leaders of the oligarchy (*Mem.* 1.2.12–14). He argues that Socrates made an immense contribution to the well-being of the

---

[57] See also Schofield 2021 on the *LP* as unwritten law.
[58] Baragwanath 2017: 280.

Athenians through his conversations with them at gymnasia and in the *agora* (1.1.10).[59] Nonetheless, the conversations Xenophon reports with Athenian craft workers such as the painter Parrhasius, the sculptor Clito, and the armourer Pistias (3.10) are as much engagements with Plato's ideas on the limits of artistic representation and mimesis as they are with Socrates' ostensible interlocutors.[60] Through these conversations, Xenophon has Socrates make claims about the possibility of representing abstract qualities in two-dimensional art (3.10.3–5) and qualities of the soul in three-dimensional art (3.10.6–8), and of the importance of fitness for purpose in manufactured tools and objects such as armour (3.10.13–15). This chapter, along with the two which precede it, offer a close engagement with Platonic ideas and suggest that Xenophon was aiming to keep track of philosophical developments. *Mem.* 3.8 depicts Socrates in conversation with Aristippus about the good and the beautiful; this discussion appears to respond to the Platonic Theory of Forms as it appears in *Republic* Book 5, showing Xenophon engaging with Plato's metaphysics.

Xenophon is at pains to present a Socrates who follows the normal practices of Athenian public and private religion (*Mem.* 1.1, 4.8). This responds both to the likely subtext of the original charges and to later writings expanding on the original accusation and defence. Although his literary defence of Socrates is not a straightforward documentation of the historical event, but a response to later discussions and publications by early Socratics and their critics, parts of the defence do provide a useful depiction of negative attitudes to law and community, and a rejection of communal values, among the Athenian elite.

Defining law

The accusers suggested that Socrates encouraged such negative attitudes in his students; Xenophon suggests rather that they were responses to the sophistic undercutting of more traditional values. The young Alcibiades attempts to demonstrate inconsistency in his guardian Pericles' understanding of the law through exploiting

---

[59] Matching Pl. *Ap.* 22de.
[60] Clearly engaging with the discussion of mimesis in Pl. *Rep.* 10.

two incompatible aspects of that understanding (*Mem.* 1.2.39–46).[61]
Pericles first suggests that laws are 'all that the people at large, after
due assembly and approval, have enacted to declare what should and
should not be done' (*Mem.* 1.2.42). Alcibiades offers counter-examples
of law under the rule of a few, or of a single person, to which the
imagined Pericles replies:

'Everything enacted by the ruling power in a state, after due consideration of what
should be done, is called law.'
  'And so even if that ruling power in the state is a tyrant, and it is he who enacts what
should be done by the citizens, is that also law?'
  'Yes, even the enactments of a tyrant in power are also called law.'
  'But, Pericles, what constitutes force and the antithesis of law? Is it not when the
stronger imposes whatever he wants on the weaker by means of force, not persuasion?'
  'I would agree with that,' said Pericles.
  'And so whatever enactments a tyrant imposes on the citizens other than by persuasion
are the antithesis of law?'
  'Yes, I agree,' said Pericles, 'and I take back my statement that whatever a tyrant enacts
without persuasion is law.'
                                                                    (*Mem.* 1.2.43–4)

Two definitions of law are in conflict: the rules set out by whoever is in
power, and the communally accepted agreements of a community.
Pericles' error, which he acknowledges, is to say that the edicts of a
tyrant constitute law. For this leads him (in real life, the most
committed of democrats) into accepting that the majority of a citizenry
can also constitute a tyranny, a key tenet of Athenian anti-democratic
thought; the idea of the 'tyranny of the majority' appears in theoretical
texts but was already well established in the mid-fifth century as a
trope of Athenian comedy.[62] By showing Alcibiades in debate with
Pericles, Xenophon perhaps anachronistically shows the continuing
development in elite Athenian thought from the strongly democratic
views of the mid-fifth century to the anti-democratic views of the period
of the war.[63]

  The *Memorabilia*'s final discussion of law emphasizes its apologetic
function, gathering evidence that Socrates' life was exemplary in its
accordance with the law (4.4.1–4), before reporting a conversation
between Socrates and Hippias of Elis, a renowned sophist visiting

---

[61] See Dorion and Bandini 2000–11: i.clx–clxix, 103–9; Danzig 2014; Johnson 2021: 95–8.
[62] See Connor 1977; Morgan 2003 (esp. Kallet 2003; Raaflaub 2003; Osborne 2003). Also
Hoekstra 2016; Lane 2016; and on tyranny more broadly, Luraghi 2015.
[63] This echoes the presentation of political conflict as intergenerational conflict, with the older
generation as the more radical, seen in Aristophanic comedy.

Athens for the first time.[64] This conversation begins to explore the idea that laws are based on the natural divine order of the cosmos, that there are 'unwritten' laws distinct from the specific, positive laws adopted by different cities. Xenophon thus stands, as some claim too for his contemporary Plato, at the beginning of an important tradition in political and legal theory, the natural law tradition.[65]

Hippias expresses dissatisfaction with Socrates' methodology, particularly his refusal to offer his own definitions but rather to proceed by attacking definitions put forward by his interlocutor. Eventually, Socrates concedes and gives a definition of the lawful, one which points back to Pericles' earlier definition (1.2.42):

'Well, I had thought that refusal to act unjustly was sufficient evidence of justice,' said Socrates. 'But if you don't agree, see whether this is more to your liking. I say that whatever is lawful (*nomimon*) is just (*dikaion*).'

'Are you saying, Socrates, that "lawful" and "just" are the same?'

'I am indeed.'

'I ask because I don't have a sense of what you mean by "lawful" or what you mean by "just".'

'You accept that cities have laws?'

'I do.'

'And what do you think they are?'

'Prescriptions agreed and enacted by the citizen body setting out what should be done and what should not be done.'

'So any citizen living his life in accordance with these prescriptions would be acting lawfully, and anyone contravening them would be acting unlawfully?'

'Certainly,' he said.

'And so anyone obeying these prescriptions would be acting justly, and anyone disobeying them would be acting unjustly?'

'Certainly.'

'Wouldn't then the man who acts justly be just, and the man who acts unjustly be unjust?'

'Of course.'

'It follows then that lawful is just, and unlawful is unjust.'

(*Mem.* 4.4.12–13)

After securing Hippias' agreement, Socrates makes a further claim, that underlying cities' positive laws are 'unwritten laws' (*agraphous...nomous*, 4.4.19), which govern personal interactions and include reverence for the

---

[64] Xenophon's presentation of Hippias echoes that of Plato; see Plato *Hippias Minor*.

[65] The Straussian tradition views classical Greek thinkers as part of the natural law tradition (see L. Strauss 1972; cf. Horky 2021); others attribute the theory of natural law's origins to later Stoic thinkers (see Long 2005).

gods, respecting parents, refraining from incest, and honouring reciprocal obligations (4.4.20–3). In some cases, breaking an unwritten law results in automatic punishment; incest, for example, results in the birth of imperfect children. Xenophon suggests that this demonstrates the divine origin of unwritten law.

Equality and distribution

The problem of distributing material goods, as well as immaterial goods such as honour, among citizens deserving of different amounts was a key preoccupation of fourth-century Greek political thought.[66] If one accepted that citizens were not actually of equal worth or status despite their formal political equality, as most Greek political thinkers did, a mechanism was needed for equitable exchange between them, both for goods and for acts of *charis*. The idea of 'geometric equality' delivered that: rather than straightforward exchanges of equal value (arithmetic equality), this concept permitted exchanges between non-equals.

However, Xenophon only touches this topic in passing in discussing Athens (*Mem.* 1.3.3, 2.4.5), exploring it in the greatest detail within the context of Cyrus' personal development (*Cyr.* 1.3), and where it relates to the distribution of the spoils of war, and of immaterial goods among them such as honour and prestige, among troops (2.2.17–24). A new geometric distribution of the spoils of battle amends the system that Cyrus had set up for organizing and rewarding his forces (2.1). Yet Cyrus faces a challenge in getting the mass meeting of soldiers to vote for the unequal distribution of rewards. In the meeting, the proposal (2.3.2–4) is backed both by the *homotimos* Chrysantas (2.3.5–6) and by a commoner, Pheraulas (2.3.8–15). In this idealized society, the interests of both elite and mass happily coincide. But Xenophon's depiction of the Persian commoners' attitude to their inferior status is idealized, and hard to apply to Athenian politics.

Collective religious action

Xenophon's portrayal of the closing stages of the Athenian civil war of 403 emphasizes the religious propriety of the democratic side, both in

---

[66] See Harvey 1965; other accounts include Arist. *Eth. Nic.* 5.3.1131a10–b24; Pl. *Leg.* 6.757b–c; Isoc. *Areopagiticus* 21–2. See also Chapters 5 and 6.

their treatment of their opponents and also in their consideration of the city's relationship with its gods, disturbed by the brutal conflict. The centrality of religion to civic identity is underscored by the powerful speech made by Cleocritus, herald of the Eleusinian Mysteries, to encourage civic reconciliation (*Hell.* 2.4.20–2).[67] He asks for peace between the factions in the name of the city's ancestral and mother gods, and the bonds of family and friendship, and begs all the citizens:

> Stop committing crimes against your fatherland, and do not obey the Thirty, the most unholy men, who in eight months have, for their private advantage, killed only a few less Athenians than all the Peloponnesians did in fighting us for ten years. Although it is possible for us to conduct our political affairs in peace, these men supply us with a war between ourselves, the most shameful of all things, and most painful and most impious and most hostile to both men and gods.   (*Hell.* 2.4.21–2)

Xenophon emphasizes the importance of these points with a string of superlative adjectives. Cleocritus, as the hereditary holder of an elite religious role, might well have been expected to side with the Thirty; Eleusis became a retreat for those who did not wish to abide by the oath of reconciliation. Although his speech fails to persuade them to seek peace, it sets the tone for the conflict which follows. The leading oligarchs are killed in battle, including Critias and Charmides, one of the board controlling the Piraeus. When the democrats gain access to the city, they process up to the Acropolis and sacrifice to the city's patron goddess, Athena (2.4.19), as if taking part in a Panathenaic procession in celebration of her birthday.

The conflict finally ends with an agreement and oath that there will be an amnesty for actions committed during the civil war. Xenophon concludes that this oath continues to be kept (2.4.43), but the trial of Socrates four years later brought that into question. Xenophon's description of Socrates' religious practice shows the ways in which citizens were expected to participate in the religious life of their *polis*. Socrates, he says, was often 'seen sacrificing either at home or at the city's communal altars' (*Mem.* 1.1.2), and he advised his friends to consult the Delphic Oracle for guidance on complex matters (1.1.6).

But, although Xenophon frequently depicts the use of oracles and sacrifices by individuals, especially at home and on campaign, he rarely depicts the collective religious life of the city. His interest is in prescribing the proper performance of religious spectacle, such as the

---

[67] Christ 2020: 28.

displays presented by the cavalry in processions and civic festivals (*Hipp.* 3.1–14; cf. *Cyr.* 8.3). Yet he emphasizes the consequences of failure to act piously: leaders and their communities can feel the long tail of divine retribution for past impiety. Xenophon attributes such retribution as a cause of the failure of Spartan hegemony in the early fourth century; events are driven by the gods' response to the Spartans' impiety in capturing Thebes' citadel (*Hell.* 5.4.1), rather than by human action or diplomacy.[68]

Leadership and the economy

It might be expected from Xenophon's *Oeconomicus* that his views on the running of households would extend to the larger-scale problem of managing a city and its finances. He has Socrates express views on the desirability of politicians understanding the practical and financial aspects of managing the city, in a series of discussions with two would-be politicians, the younger Pericles (*Mem.* 3.5) and Glaucon (3.6), and one older Athenian, Charmides (3.7). Xenophon's choice of interlocutors for Socrates here suggests an engagement with Plato's work. Unlike Plato, he regards a practical command of finance essential to good government, and so, at the level of the city, as at the level of the citizen, he is concerned that good decisions and actions are taken involving money.

   Xenophon also addresses the ideological aversion to engagement with finance that went with the quietist anti-democratic views with which he is otherwise aligned. He shows Ischomachus as a leading citizen actively engaged with business and finance (*Oec.* 7.1–2). And he has Socrates criticize young Athenians for failing to learn about economic matters (*Mem.* 3.5–6). For Matthew Christ, this pragmatic insistence that the elite should participate in the management of the city's economy shows Xenophon's realistic engagement with the issues of Athenian democracy.[69]

   Xenophon's concerns are also those of the fourth-century context in which he was writing, rather than the fifth-century Athens of Socrates' later life. The financial management of the *polis* had become a preoccupation of the democracy, and new roles requiring specialist

---

[68] Tuplin 1993; Dillery 1995. See also Chapter 5.
[69] Christ 2020: 72–3.

expertise offered a path to civic honour for politicians such as Eubulus and Lycurgus.[70] Eubulus, who held the elected office of treasurer in Athens during the 350s, is said to have sponsored the lifting of the decree of exile against Xenophon (DL 2.56).

Socrates' discussion with the aspiring politician Glaucon reflects this concern. The young Glaucon has been trying to establish himself in politics, but has been ridiculed when he has spoken in public, and Socrates tries to show why this has happened:

So now Socrates continued, saying, 'Well, Glaucon, one obvious point is that if you want to win all that honour you must do some good (ōphelētea) to the city. Is that not so?'

'Absolutely,' he said.

'Well, come on then,' said Socrates, 'don't keep it to yourself, but tell us what will be the first thing you will do for the good of the city (euergetein)?'

When Glaucon fell silent, as if this was the first time he had had to think about where to begin, Socrates said, 'If it was your aim to extend a friend's family holding, you would set about making him wealthier (plousiōteron). Will you in the same way try to make the city wealthier?'

'Absolutely,' he said.

'And the city would be wealthier if it had more sources of revenue?'

'I guess so,' he said.

'Tell me, then,' said Socrates, 'what the city's present sources of revenue are, and how much they bring in. Obviously you will have looked into this, so that you can boost any that are failing and exploit any missed opportunities.'

'Well no, frankly,' said Glaucon, 'I haven't looked into that.'

(Mem. 3.6.3–5)

Socrates insists that good service to the *polis* involves improving its financial resources. The elite should enable the city to generate wealth in the same way that a well-run private estate might, as a form of euergetism. This requires specialist expertise: knowledge of income, expenditure, and potential sources for improvement to both. Given the use of Plato's brother as interlocutor, it is hard not to read this as Xenophon's critique of Plato's valorization of more abstract knowledge. Glaucon makes a policy suggestion, increasing reparations levied on enemies (3.6.7), but Socrates' careful questioning reveals his ignorance about the city's current military and financial position.

Xenophon strongly advocated having a firm grasp on resources and finance. Towards the end of his life, he offered his advice to the city,

---

[70] For fourth-century context, see Whitehead 2019; Cartledge 2016.

then impoverished by defeat in the Social War of 357–355.[71] His short pamphlet, *Poroi* ('Revenues'), considers ways in which Athens might boost its economy and increase revenues. Philippe Gauthier and others have argued that Xenophon aims to solidify political order, rather than encourage economic growth as a goal in its own right. Matthew Christ adds that Xenophon's arguments here reshape elite engagement with the city.[72]

In the *Poroi*, Xenophon offers a realistic assessment of Athens' current strengths and weaknesses. He suggests ways of extracting more revenue from different sectors of the economy. This includes the more efficient exploitation of the economic and military capacity of resident non-citizens (metics), while at the same time improving their engagement with the city (*Poroi* 2.1–7). The aim is to preserve the existing order.[73]

This plan extends to the enslaved population of the city. Xenophon notes that those holding leases on the silver mines have enjoyed better returns when they have invested in increasing the enslaved workforce labouring on extracting silver (4.14). He suggests that, once a public fund has been raised by a peacetime tax on wealthy citizens, the money can be invested in enterprises such as building a workforce of enslaved labourers who can be leased to citizens, enabling improved productivity and returns on mining leases (4.18–26), and building a pool of economic resources such as merchant ships (3.14). All citizens would benefit from this new fund; all citizens would receive a daily three-obol allowance from it (3.8–9); wealthy citizens would also benefit from the availability of labour resources to make their own enterprises more productive.

The purpose of this increase in economic activity is to make peace pay and reduce the need to go to war to capture resources, a risk which the city cannot currently afford. For Xenophon, economic activity is sustained by peace, and vice versa. Athens' location, and its established port facilities, mean that it is a hub for trade across the Greek world in both material goods and immaterial ones such as education and theatrical production (1.6–7, 5.3–4).[74] Building a

[71] Whitehead 2019: 7–12; Bloch 2004.
[72] Gauthier 1976: 21; Christ 2020: 143.
[73] Whitehead 2019: 38–9.
[74] Farrell 2016; Whitehead 2019: 7–12.

peacetime economy would solidify Athens' status more effectively than attempting to dominate other cities through war.

Although this is a radically different policy from that which Athens had been pursuing, and failing at, Xenophon is at pains to show that it would enable a restoration of the city and its traditional arrangements (6.1). Although Eubulus and Xenophon could possibly have been in contact, there is little evidence of Eubulus taking up these plans in his own administration.[75] However, David Whitehead has argued that the policies of a later politician, Lycurgus (who administered the city c.336–324), do seem to reflect Xenophon's suggestions made two decades previously.[76] An example is the leasing of public land at the Piraeus to non-Greek Cypriot merchants from Citium to build their own temple, proposed by Lycurgus and agreed in an assembly resolution in 333/2 BCE.[77] Lycurgus' policies need not necessarily have been influenced by Xenophon, and Athens' situation in the 330s, after defeat by the Macedonians at Chaeronea in 338, was even less strong than it had been in the 350s. But the similarity between Xenophon's proposals and the decisions made by Athens at this later point suggests that his ideas were not out of line with those of the city's administrators.

Conclusion

The question of what constitutes good government at the scale of the city is central to many of Xenophon's works. He found answers in idealized versions of the arrangements of Sparta, including those he presented as a Persian *politeia*. He praises arrangements where traditional values are upheld – or at least those values currently considered traditional – and where change is difficult to implement. Although he criticizes the changeability of Athenian law under the democratic regime, his account of the excesses of the Thirty shows that he recognizes that extremism is a vice at both ends of the political spectrum. While Sparta and Persia exemplify his long-standing ideals, he takes a practical interest in the immediate problems of Athens.

[75] Whitehead 2019: 21–30 contra Cawkwell 1963; cf. Gauthier 1976: 223–31.
[76] Whitehead 2019: 42–52.
[77] RO 91 = *IG* II² 337.

V. ON CAMPAIGN

From the *Iliad* onwards, Greek writers treated military camps as analogues of political communities, with their hierarchical structures and mass assemblies, places where generals shared plans with their troops and occasionally faced their criticism. Xenophon's exploration of order and leadership finds the military context a fruitful one.

His narratives of military campaigns feature his most vivid and lively writing, and some of his most personal reflections. His own experience enlivens the narrative of the *Anabasis*, the failed expedition to place Cyrus the Younger on the Achaemenid throne, in which he participated (401 BCE), and sharpens his analysis of episodes in the *Hellenica* such as the Spartan campaigns led by Agesilaus in Asia Minor (396–394) and on the Greek mainland (394 onwards). Xenophon's accounts of these events are shaped to provide exemplary narratives of leadership; Shane Brennan notes that in the *Anabasis* Xenophon himself appears 'more like an exemplar than a historical figure'.[1] The *Anabasis* is both a 'microhistory' of a specific campaign (Flower), and a patterned exemplary narrative which is 'part military handbook, part ethnography, part retrospective self-justification' (Lee).[2]

For Xenophon, the army is a location in which leadership skill and the capacity to create order can be demonstrated. Both the *Anabasis* and the more idealized *Cyropaedia*, with its account of Cyrus the Great's rise to power through conquest, contain theorizing about spatial organization, as applicable to the city as the camp.[3] The army is also a kind of *polis* on the move; given that cities' armies were still made up, for the most part, of their citizens, and military leaders often had political clout, this was self-evident and demonstrated in the similarity between assemblies of troops and those of citizens. The camp and the *polis* become interchangeable.

Just as with the city, Xenophon is focused on the challenges facing the elite, generals and those who wish to be generals. His Socratic works are perhaps surprisingly concerned with Athenian military leadership (*Mem.* 3.1–5), but his most detailed account of a programme of military training and organization in the field is delivered in the

---

[1] Brennan 2022: 2.
[2] Lee 2008: 4; Flower 2012: 47–8.
[3] On expeditionary forces as *polis*-like entities, see Hornblower 2004.

Cyropaedia. He is clear that the aim of good military leadership is the same as that of civic leadership, as Socrates says:

Why do you think Homer called Agamemnon 'shepherd of the people'? Is it because the shepherd must see to it that his sheep are safe and have what they need, so that the purpose for which they are kept is achieved? And in the same way must the general see to it that his troops are safe and have what they need, so that the purpose for which they campaign is achieved – that purpose being to win a happier life by defeating the enemy?   (*Mem.* 3.2.1)

The goals of warfare are aligned with the wider need for management. Military leaders should pursue the well-being of both their forces and those they protect. Xenophon emphasizes the importance of the former, detailing arrangements for quartering, feeding, and training forces, and treating logistics as a core leadership skill. However, his accounts of campaigns are not simply programmatic or patterned, but full of incidental detail. As well as set-piece battle narratives, he reports interactions between Greek forces and the peoples they encounter, schemes to train and improve troops, and dissent and disagreement among forces. Above all, the army represents an ordered community.

Xenophon's interest in orderliness and ordering, seen in his account of the household (Chapter 3), applies to armies on and off the battlefield. Although his Socrates insists that this is only a small part of leadership, Xenophon acknowledges its importance; as his Ischomachus says, 'an orderly army is the finest sight for its friends' (*Oec.* 8.6). Xenophon is particularly concerned with *taxis*, the make-up and arrangement of forces, whether on the battlefield, in transit, or in camp. This preoccupies him as the Cyreans try to find a practical arrangement for their large group and appropriate protection for their journey across hostile terrain (*An.* 3.3.15–19, 3.4.19–23, 4.4.28–9).[4] Xenophon expands on this in the *Cyropaedia*, showing the earlier Cyrus encouraging innovative arrangements and rewarding those who trained their men to deploy them (*Cyr.* 2.3.21–2); his own innovations and willingness to send out cavalry scouts from the main column had not always been well received. Cavalry as well as infantry forces benefit from good arrangement, both in battle and as sources of civic spectacle (*Hipp.* 2.2–9, 3.3–13).

A well-organized military camp already instantiates civic communal activity, such as messes and physical training. On occasion, an army

---

[4] Lee 2008: 141–7.

and its city can become the same entity. When the small Peloponnesian city of Phlius is besieged, Xenophon praises its leading citizens' commitment to their alliance with Sparta as they see off a challenge from democratic exiles (*Hell.* 7.2).[5] The character of the leading citizens is attributed to the city as a collective.

Xenophon regards the Cyreans as a community with the potential to settle and to realize itself as a *polis* (*An.* 5.6.15), and even identifies their camp at Calpe as a good location for this transformation, close to the sea (6.4.8). John Dillery traces the narrative arc of the *Anabasis* as the sudden restructuring of this potential community, through a brief period of social coherence, on to its gradual disintegration.[6] Discord in the camp echoes stasis within a *polis*, and Xenophon's plans did not find favour. In the same way, friendship and erotic relationships between men on campaign echo those they might have pursued at home.

The *Cyropaedia* provides Xenophon with a space in which his ideals can be realized, albeit in fiction. The elder Cyrus' changes to the Persian army and his ideas on the organization and management of armies can also be read as comment on the structure and leadership of political communities. Cyrus himself created the best order in his camps in his progress around his empire (*Cyr.* 8.5.1–15); again, these create an ordered community within which the leader is protected from potential harm, and where quick mobilization is possible.

Battle scenes and their rhetoric

Leaders face critical moments in preparing for battle, mustering and ordering their troops, and maintaining control on the battlefield. Xenophon's battle narratives, however, are not attempts to document the action – many battles were far too diffuse and confused for that to be possible – but opportunities for a range of rhetorical flourishes which contribute to the building of character portraits.

His account of the battle of Cunaxa, in which Cyrus the Younger was killed, exemplifies the incompleteness of his narratives, which has frustrated modern historians; it 'simply will not do', according to Cawkwell.[7] Battle narratives typically begin with a list of forces and

---

[5] Dillery 1995: 130–8.
[6] Dillery 1995: 77–90.
[7] Warner and Cawkwell 1972: 19.

their planned arrangement. Xenophon details the sizes of the forces (*An.* 1.7.10–13), but his numbers for the Persians, led by Cyrus' older full brother Artaxerxes II, are implausibly large.[8] His account of the key manoeuvres of the opposing forces contains inconsistencies, perhaps unsurprisingly, given the difficulty of securing an accurate overview of complex events taking place across a large area, but it does provide a vivid account of the charge and fighting which led to Cyrus' death (1.8.24–7). Here Xenophon admits that he draws on another account, that of Artaxerxes' Greek doctor Ctesias (1.8.26), to provide details of events on the battlefield that he could not see for himself.[9] Even the moment of Cyrus' death marks the otherness of the Persians; whether by his own hand or in defence of his master's body, Cyrus' sceptre-bearer lies dead beside his master (1.8.28–9), evoking an orientalist trope which reappears in the story of the Asian queen Pantheia (see Chapter 6).[10]

Xenophon uses commanders' addresses to their troops to convey his own analysis and to provide enjoyable and inspiring examples of rhetoric.[11] Cyrus' address to his Greek troops before Cunaxa emphasizes recurring Xenophontic themes:

I have taken you on for this reason, that I believe you to be better and stronger than many barbarians. See to it, therefore, that you are worthy of the freedom (*eleutherias*) which you hold, on account of which I consider you to be happy. Be assured that I would choose freedom in place of all that I have and many multiples of it.

(*An.* 1.7.3)

Battle speeches, whether to the whole army or to the commanding officers, also feature heavily in the *Cyropaedia*; even the earlier Cyrus' first speech, to the small force of 1,000 men he takes from Persia to support the Medes against the Assyrians, runs through familiar points about the virtues of practice and self-discipline, respect for the gods, and the justice of their cause (*Cyr.* 1.5.7–14).[12] But as Cyrus observes, such speeches must activate the qualities already present in their audience; they cannot improve forces which lack training, discipline, or a framework of laws to follow (*Cyr.* 3.3.49–55).

---

[8] Compare Herodotus on the Persians, Hdt. 7.60.
[9] Ctesias F20 = Plut. *Vit. Artax.* 11–13. See Anderson 1974: 98–112; Bigwood 1983.
[10] Degen 2020.
[11] Rood 2004a; Tuplin 2014.
[12] See also *Cyr.* 3.3.34–9, 41–2; 6.2.14–20; 7.5.20–24; for addresses to officers, see *Cyr.* 2.4.22–9, 4.1.2–6.

Xenophon's account of the Athenian naval battle at Arginusae (*Hell.* 1.6.26–35; see Chapter 4) has led to speculation that he participated in it, perhaps as a marine, but the description is shaped to his own narrative needs.[13] Although Xenophon details the political and military manoeuvres which preceded the battle, including the Athenian dispatch of additional triremes to the scene, his account of the conflict itself is perfunctory, with only one short section narrating the events of the lengthy battle (1.6.33). His interest lies in the disaster after the battle, when both confusion and a storm prevented the Athenians from rescuing sailors from sinking ships – necessary background information to his subsequent account of the trial.

Another important battle narrative is that of Coronea (394 BCE), in which Agesilaus' Spartan forces, along with allies from Phocis and Orchomenos, confronted a broad alliance of Greek forces from Thebes, Athens, Argos, Corinth, and beyond (*Ages.* 2.6). For once, Xenophon's account of this battle does not resort to exaggerated numbers, as the balance in number and capability between the forces is key. Instead, he shows how perceptions of the battle differed: Agesilaus' mercenaries thought it was over, but a late charge by the Thebans broke through another part of the battle line. Agesilaus was wounded in a courageous counter-charge requiring a skilled turnaround of his forces (2.10–11) – 'brave, but not very safe', Xenophon notes – which eventually secured victory. Xenophon suggests the brutality of the combat with a terse series of verbs: 'they thrust their shields out and were pushing, fighting, killing, dying' (2.12). His description of the bloody aftermath of this battle between Greek cities is haunting, a string of perfect-tense participles emphasizing the permanence of the destruction:

When the battle had ceased, it was possible to observe a spectacle (*theasasthai*), where men had fallen with each other to the earth reddened with blood (*pephurmenēn*), corpses of friends and enemies lying together, shields crushed (*diatethrummenas*), spears broken into pieces (*suntethrausmena*), knives bare of their sheaths, some on the ground, some in bodies, and others still in their hands.   (*Ages.* 2.14)

As Rosie Harman observes, Xenophon's description 'is not focalised from any one position' and does not take sides.[14] Even in a work praising the Spartan king with whom he had served, Xenophon holds

[13] See Chapter 2.
[14] Harman 2008: 440–1.

back from exulting in a scene in which fellow Greeks – and possibly Athenians – were among the dead and suffering. If Coronea was the occasion which confirmed his exile from Athens, his reticence is understandable.

Xenophon as a soldier and leader

While some readings of the *Anabasis* have emphasized narrative and adventure, two quite different recent readings, by Shane Brennan and Eric Buzzetti, explore it as a case study in 'Socratic' leadership.[15] Xenophon may exaggerate his own role in the expedition; some have suggested that he responds to other, now lost, accounts, but the fragmentary evidence makes it hard to ascertain the realities.[16] Given the patterning of Xenophon's work more broadly, no aspect can be treated as a straightforward narrative. His description of his role plays out aspects of his idealization of leadership.[17] Xenophon uses the critical battle in which Cyrus the Younger was killed, the battle of Cunaxa (*An.* 1.8.1–1.10.19), to introduce himself as a character into his own narrative with a pious action suggestive of courage (1.8.15).

The experience of the mixed mercenary forces who made up the Cyreans on the Persian campaign gave Xenophon insight into different leadership styles and approaches to battlefield tactics, as well as the broader management of an army in hostile territory. He presents the restructuring of the Cyreans after the loss of Cyrus and their generals through a series of speeches which Xenophon himself gives to progressively larger groups of different status, starting with his motivational speech to himself in which he expresses his determination to survive (3.1.11–14).[18] The speeches of Xenophon and others are punctuated by divine signs: the dream which first inspires Xenophon to take action; and a sneeze just after two of the remaining leaders have spoken to the assembled Greek soldiers (3.2.9), when Xenophon is about to persuade the men that it is possible to return, and to set out his plan for doing so.

---

[15] Buzzetti 2014; Brennan 2022.

[16] The story that Xenophon was responding to a written account by Sophaenetus, 'the oldest of the generals' (6.5.13), is an ancient one, though rejected by Brennan (2022: 4). Other accounts include DS 14.25–31 (summarizing Ephorus' lost account), Plut. *Vit. Artax.* 6–14, Ctesias' fragmentary *Persica*, and DL 2.49–51; see Brennan and Thomas 2021: 420–52.

[17] Due 1989: 203–6.

[18] Atack 2022.

As a speaker, Xenophon develops a distinctive rhetoric for the different audience, developing and amplifying details in each iteration.

A low point of Xenophon's own military experience was a court-martial for *hubris*, inappropriate violence toward subordinates (*An.* 5.8.2), after one of the Cyreans accused him of assault during the group's struggle to progress through snow, when Xenophon lost his temper with the stragglers (4.5.16). While many aspects of Xenophon's account of his adventures with the Cyreans are idealized and shaped as exemplars, and he generally puts a positive spin on his own contributions, his own failings as a leader and his difficulties in communicating with and managing troops eventually emerge from the narrative. In many ways, he exhibits the same failings as he attributes to his friend Proxenus. He struggles to persuade the group to accept his relentless stream of good ideas, and his relationship with the forces deteriorates as the journey continues. Episodes where the troops are distrustful of his motivation and critical of his actions culminate in his being put on trial. Michael Flower notes that these episodes structure the narrative, creating sections (corresponding to book divisions) in which Xenophon faces a new danger.[19] Another recurring theme is Xenophon's reluctance to take on a formal leadership role, even when it is offered to him; he finds evidence from the gods, via sacrifice, that he should not become the group's formal leader (6.1.31).

Xenophon's practicality is seen most clearly in his concern with the provisioning of troops and their animals, expressed in his initial plan to bring them home (3.2.34) and continuing throughout the journey. His works on training emphasize the importance of maintaining men and animals in good health; there is a mean between uncontrolled appetite and starvation which ensures peak physical performance (*LP* 2.5–7).[20]

The Cyreans must balance their need for food and supplies with the difficulties of transporting and storing bulky goods. One of Xenophon's first suggestions is that they minimize what they take with them. As he outlines the risks of their forthcoming journey, he urges them to destroy surplus possessions so that they are not held up by a baggage train (*An.* 3.2.27–8). However, the need to forage on the journey provokes conflict with the peoples whose territory they cross, and demonstrates the difficult trade-off that Xenophon had attempted to negotiate.

---

[19] Flower 2012: 141.
[20] Humble 2022: 105.

Xenophon's assessment of other military leaders

Xenophon's self-portrait in the *Anabasis* is accompanied by other exemplary portraits of leadership, which he delivers through his narrative, through speeches which act as manifestos (such as his own addresses to the surviving Cyrean captains and troops, *An.* 3.2), and through authorial comment. Diphridas the Spartan, for example, 'was no less charming (*eucharis*) than Thibron' (his colleague) but 'a more organized and enterprising general', who set aside bodily pleasures and got on with his job (*Hell.* 4.8.22). The Spartan naval leader Teleutias supports his half-brother Agesilaus in a raid on Corinth (4.4.19), and then drives the Athenians away from Aegina (5.1.1–3). While none of his actions are of great strategic significance, Xenophon finds him noteworthy because of the way he inspires and motivates his troops (5.1.4). Jason, the tyrant of Pherae, appears as an exemplar in a speech given by Polydamas of Pharsalus (also in Thessaly) as he appeals for Spartan support (6.1.4–19). Polydamas attests to Jason's own personal physical excellence and concern for training his forces, and reports the skilled speech with which Jason attempted to persuade the Pharsalians to support him. With Jason presented as an exemplary leader in both speech and action, Xenophon returns to him a couple of chapters later, by which time he has come to dominate Thessaly (6.4.28). But he is assassinated while preparing for a festival, a final pious act that secures Xenophon's approval.

After the critical juncture of the younger Cyrus' death on the battlefield of Cunaxa near Babylon (*An.* 1.8), and the subsequent capture and execution of the Greek generals Clearchus, Proxenus, and Meno (2.5.27–31, 2.6.1), Xenophon pays tribute to each, providing a gallery of leadership types similar to the presentation of Athenian politicians in *Hellenica* 2. As Michael Flower noted, the obituaries also 'offer a sort of benchmark by which to measure Xenophon himself after he becomes one of the new generals'.[21] He sympathizes with the complex situations which led the generals to abandon service to their own cities, but criticizes their distinctive failings even as he points out their admirable qualities, shaping his portraits carefully.

---

[21] Flower 2012: 103.

The Spartan general Clearchus (*An.* 2.6.1–15) loved warfare (*philopolemos*) to the extent that it unbalanced his decision-making. Xenophon fails to mention that the Spartans exiled him after he refused to end a campaign.[22] Clearchus comes across as a disturbingly violent man, who is quick to administer corporal punishment to weaker soldiers; he beats one of Meno's soldiers, provoking a violent dispute within the Greek forces (*An.* 1.5.11–17). Xenophon admires Clearchus' ability to secure obedience, reporting his brusque, stereotypically Spartan, addresses to his troops (1.3.7–9). Some scholars have thought him critical of Clearchus' harshness; others that he is more sympathetic to a character who displays signs of what might now be identified as a combatant's post-traumatic stress disorder.[23] Clearchus' ready brutality prepares the reader for similar behaviour from his successor, Cheirisophus (4.6.1–3).

Proxenus of Boeotia, the guest-friend (*xenos*) who recruited Xenophon to the expedition, fails to connect with his troops, despite his personal excellence and assiduous study of rhetoric (*An.* 2.6.16–20). His encouragement through praise produces positive results only with men of good character, *kaloi kagathoi*; he cannot motivate or secure good behaviour from the mass of troops. Xenophon closes his short assessment of Proxenus with the note that he was thirty years old when he was killed – likely little older than Xenophon himself at the time (2.6.20). When Xenophon effectively takes over Proxenus' role as leader of the Greek contingent among the Cyreans, he demonstrates similar failings.

Xenophon is severely critical of Meno of Thessaly, contrasting his bad character with that of Proxenus (*An.* 2.6.21–9).[24] While Proxenus had most influence over the virtuous, Meno leads by appealing to the worst of his men and using 'oath-breaking, lying and deception' in pursuit of his goals of wealth, power, and honour. Meno laughs at the honest and regards them as 'uneducated' (*apaideutōn*, 2.6.26), lacking the sophistication that an elite education might bring. Xenophon suggests that he acquired his leadership role through favouritism, and adds further hints of sexual impropriety in same-sex relationships which fell beyond the accepted bounds and

---

[22] Laforse 2000.

[23] Critical, Roisman 1989; empathetic, Tritle 2004: 326–9.

[24] The presence of Meno, Socrates' interlocutor in Plato's *Meno*, and that of Socrates, connect the *Anabasis* to Platonic dialogue: see Nails 2002: 204–5.

suggested uncontrolled appetites (2.6.28).[25] Meno had demonstrated his lack of commitment to process and collaborative decision-making when the Greeks were discussing whether to support Cyrus' campaign. He took his contingent across the river to join Cyrus while the other Greeks were still debating what to do, perhaps seeking to secure special personal favour as the first to join the expedition (1.4.17).

These disparate portraits of leadership separate the two halves of the story of the expedition and provide a framework for understanding how the new leaders, including Xenophon himself, perform as the surviving Cyreans attempt to escape to safety, travelling from Babylon over the mountains to the Black Sea coast.

Xenophon opens the *Cyropaedia* with an assessment of Cyrus the Great's own capacity as a leader (*Cyr.* 1.1.3–6), using the subsequent narrative to show those qualities developing. He depicts the young Cyrus pushing against the boundaries as he seeks to move from hunting expeditions contained within the royal park (1.4.5–6), to hunting in wilder country (1.4.14–15), to fighting human enemies encroaching on prime hunting land, and demonstrating his courage and military skill for the first time (1.4.16–24).[26] Cyrus' first initiatives are quick responses to opportunities which place him and his companions in unacceptable danger. As his forces grow and the stakes are increased, picking the right moment to pursue enemies or to engage in battle becomes more important. Recognizing such moments is a matter of grasping the *kairos*, a skill Xenophon values highly; Cyrus' supreme ability in this respect sets him apart from the other military leaders Xenophon depicts, including himself.[27]

Xenophon's most detailed, if perhaps least critical, assessment of a contemporary figure is of the Spartan king Agesilaus. The central section of the *Hellenica* narrates Agesilaus' campaign in Asia Minor, in which Xenophon himself participated, and his later campaign on the Greek mainland. Xenophon also revisits Agesilaus' career in his short obituary, the *Agesilaus*. The *Hellenica* account shares themes with the *Anabasis*: portraits of military leaders at key moments, and the conflict between Spartan and other cultures and values. But the *Agesilaus* provides an idealized portrait of its subject, often described vividly, as

---

[25] Dover 2016: 87. See also Chapter 3, pp. 41–5, on homosociality.
[26] Cf. Vidal-Naquet 1968.
[27] Atack 2018b; Trédé 1992.

the king's piety and management of an appropriate relationship with
the gods are in one scene from his camp at Ephesus:

Anyone would have been encouraged by seeing first Agesilaus and then all the other
soldiers when then came back from their exercise wearing garlands, and dedicated
the garlands to Artemis. For where men show due honour to the gods, train in the skills
of war, and take care to develop their obedience to command (*peitharchian*), is it not
reasonable in these circumstances for everything to be full of good hopes?

(*Ages.* 1.27)

This recalls Xenophon's own portrait of sacrifices to Artemis at the
estate in Scillous on which he settled after this campaign (*An.* 5.3.7–
13; see Chapter 3).

Xenophon reports with approval the many occasions on which
leaders sacrifice to discover the will of the gods before taking important
actions, especially crossing borders and rivers. The leaders of the Ten
Thousand perform sacrifices before setting off on their return journey,
to ensure that they do so at the right time (*hōras*, *An.* 3.5.18), and at
difficult moments along the way. When they are struggling to find a
way to ford the river Centrites, favourable sacrifices confirm the
omens that Xenophon has experienced in a dream (4.3.8). Soon
afterwards, Xenophon is told of a crossing place by two of the soldiers;
he takes care to pour libations to the gods in thanks, and to perform
further sacrifices to confirm that it is the right time to cross (4.3.17).

Xenophon's emphasis on the use of sacrifice and divination is not
just an expression of piety. Leaders' ability to engage with the divine
enables them both to gather information not accessible by other
means and also to demonstrate to their followers that they have the
support of the gods.[28] For Agesilaus and Cyrus, the ability to acquire
and use information from the gods demonstrates their royal authority
(see Chapter 6). But other leaders too, notably Xenophon himself,
use religious practice as a key resource for information gathering and
determining when and how to act.

Military training in Sparta, Athens, and Persia

Xenophon's philosophy of self-management, extending to taking care
of the development of self and others, is a natural fit for – and may

---

[28] Durnerin 2022.

even have originated in – his experiences on campaign, interpreted through the lens of his Socratic education. Training and discipline are the keys to success. These ideas are voiced by Socrates as Xenophon depicts him discussing preparation for leadership with ambitious young Athenians. When one of his associates considers studying generalship with a visiting expert, Dionysodorus, Socrates approves:[29]

That's because in the dangers of war the whole city is dependent on the general, and great good or great harm can come from his success or failure. So wouldn't it be right to penalize someone who puts himself up for election without bothering to learn how to do the job?   (*Mem.* 3.1.3)

The nature and content of training is important. Socrates insists that tactics, the focus of Dionysodorus' lessons, are only a small part of generalship:

A general must also be able to procure the resources for war and arrange for the provisioning of his troops; he must be inventive, energetic, focused, hardy, and quick-witted; capable of being both benign and brutal, both frank and devious, both watchman and thief, both lavish and grasping, both generous and greedy, equally good at defence and attack – and there are many other qualities, either natural or taught, which are needed by someone who wants to be a successful general.   (*Mem.* 3.1.6)

Socrates goes on to consider how one might determine which are the stronger and weaker parts of an army, a dimension crucial to planning deployment on the battlefield.[30] This discussion offers a practical instance of the problem of the nature of excellence, central to the Socratic dialogue.

Xenophon returns to specific points in the subsequent conversations. Pericles' son wants to become a politician and general and to make his mark on the city, but lacks experience (*Mem.* 3.5).[31] After discussing the city's changing situation and the attitudes of its citizens to leaders, Socrates suggests a specific tactical intervention, using youths as light-armed troops to raid the mountainous border with Boeotia (3.5.25–7). This detail might seem like the record of a real conversation, but this location, and style of campaign, fit the time of Xenophon's

---

[29] It is unclear whether this Dionysodorus is the twin sophist of Plato's *Euthydemus*, or simply named to evoke him; see Nails 2002: 136–7.
[30] Xenophon reprises this theme at *Cyr.* 1.6.12–15.
[31] McNamara 2009.

writing (possibly the 360s or 350s) rather than the dramatic date (before 406, when Pericles was one of the generals at Arginusae).

The views which Xenophon gives to Socrates suggest his approval of collectively organized military training. Again, this was a concern of Athens in Xenophon's time, not Socrates'. The Spartan education regime offered one model in which all learning was oriented towards this goal; Xenophon describes these arrangements with approval (*LP* 2.7).

Cavalry

Xenophon's military advice often reflects his interest and experience in the cavalry. He even depicts Socrates, known to have served as a hoplite, giving out advice on the management of horses and their riders to a newly elected cavalry commander (*Mem.* 3.3). Socrates' advice starts from the general principle that the role of the commander is to leave his forces 'in better condition after your tenure' (3.3.2), and concludes with the broadly applicable points that the commander must inspire those he leads with his own excellence (3.3.8–9), and be able to speak to them persuasively (3.3.10). He insists that the commander is responsible for both the riders and their mounts, rather than each soldier's being responsible for his own horses (3.3.3–4). Socrates' advice, though applied to this specific context, is no different from Xenophon's usual framework of good leadership activities.

Xenophon offers further specific advice to the Athenians in the *Hipparchicus*, a short instructional work intended to help a cavalry officer perform well, and which exemplifies his belief in the importance of public service. Here he does cover highly specific and technical ground, while reiterating familiar points; Paul Cartledge notes that Xenophon's interest in the cavalry at the likely composition date may have been intensified by his son's service.[32] The work is the clearest statement of Xenophon's views on military leadership. Although he starts by advising that the commander should begin by sacrificing and asking the advice of the gods (*Hipp.* 1.1), he moves quickly to the practical question of recruitment (1.2). In the end, he recommends enlisting foreign riders to keep the cavalry forces up to strength, along

---

[32] Cartledge and Waterfield 1997: 66.

with wealthy resident aliens (9.3–7), a need which might point to the difficulties of Athens in this area in the mid-fourth century.[33]

Xenophon prioritizes the care of the horses and the need to ensure adequate nutrition for all, and the logistics this involves on campaign. His suggestions for the organization of hierarchies of command and battlefield formation (*Hipp.* 2.1–9), and for training exercises reinforced by prizes and rewards (1.26), echo the more idealized training plans of Cyrus. In the context of Athens, these structures feed into the agonistic culture of the elite, where leading citizens might compete for rewards in producing the best-trained horsemen under their command, just as they did for choruses. That is not the only similarity drawn with the production of choruses: Xenophon acknowledges (3.1–14) that cavalry commanders were also responsible for contributing teams of riders to processions and festivals (as seen on the Parthenon frieze). He is particularly keen that they should be able to demonstrate skills in galloping and charging in such public displays. As Ben Keim notes, the treatise is oriented towards a culture in which personal honour is highly valued.

Cyrus the Great and the organization of training

Xenophon creates an idealized training regime in his depiction of the older Cyrus working relentlessly to improve his forces, instigating training, setting up prizes to reward skill, and redirecting whole groups to gain new skills to expand the overall capacity and capability of the Persians. Some of these interventions had radical implications for Persian society, as commentators have noted. Xenophon's Persia, like the Greek *polis*, features the close association of military role with class status: the division between the elite 'peers' of the leisure class and the ordinary Persians who must work for a living.[34] While the narrative describes Cyrus' reorganization of his forces, it also offers a case study in ideas about equitable distribution among a diverse citizen body, a central concern of Greek political thinking.[35]

The first reorganization eliminates a key status distinction in the army.[36] At the beginning of Cyrus' campaign, the distinction between

---

[33] Keim 2018.
[34] Nadon 2001: 39–40.
[35] See Harvey 1965; other accounts include Arist. *Eth. Nic.* 5.3.1131a10–b24; Pl. *Leg.* 6.757b–c; Isoc. *Areopagiticus* 21–2.
[36] Gray 2011b: 283–8.

peers and commoners echoes that of Athenian forces, with poorer citizens and non-citizen troops fighting with lighter weaponry and distance weapons such as bows and slingshots, and the wealthier citizen hoplite elite wearing body armour and bearing bladed weapons. Xenophon has already shown how Persian society divides those of citizen status between those who undergo the state education and become a leisure class of 'peers', and those whose families cannot afford this and who must work for a living (see pp. 58–9). Cyrus collapses this division in his forces by equipping the commoners with armour and bladed weapons, so that they can participate in hand-to-hand combat (*Cyr.* 2.1.9). His uncle Cyaxares has explained the size of the enemy force approaching the Medians and their allies; Cyrus appears to find it difficult to report the low number of Persian peers on their way to join the camp, and suggests this change as a means of expanding the battle-field capabilities of the combined forces. The move also resembles a policy that Xenophon attributes to the Spartans (*LP* 11.3), of giving all their forces a uniform and shield so that the whole force looks the same, and skill or status distinctions become invisible.[37]

This remarkable change is analysed through the subsequent narrative and debates.[38] By redistributing weaponry, Cyrus has disrupted the status hierarchy in Persian society. The commoners and the 'peers' become equal in some respects. Cyrus explains to the peers that their role is as exemplars to those taking up arms for the first time, and stresses that they will display their own excellence by taking responsibility for those they lead (*Cyr.* 2.1.11). In this way, he leaves some room for them to maintain a superior position in the hierarchy as commanders.

Meanwhile, Cyrus emphasizes to the commoners that they differ from the peers only in their need to earn a living, that they are not lesser in body or worse in soul (2.1.14). In taking up weapons for close-range fighting, they will take on the same risks, as well as potential rewards. They will be 'considered worthy of the same as us' and provided with an income, or at least the necessities of life, in return for their new role (2.1.14). The assembled commoners all accept the offer and begin their training with their new weapons (2.1.19–20).

Parallel changes in Athenian democracy – the opening up of political office to all citizen classes – were criticized by other fourth-century political theorists, such as Aristotle, whose discussions in his *Politics*

---

[37] Humble 2022: 165–8.
[38] Nadon 2001: 61–76; Gray 2011b: 283–5.

cover very similar terrain to Xenophon's.[39] Xenophon acknowledges that the lack of leisure time to devote to self-development, the key complaint about poorer citizens, has affected the light-armed troops' ability to train. Cyrus aims to provide them with the time and resources for this. However, Xenophon interleaves his description of Cyrus' arrangements for organizing the new troops, training them, and motivating them to do well (2.1.22–4) with comic episodes which explore the tension created by the change of status of the commoners. First, the ineptitude of some of the commoners in training is exemplified by comic misunderstanding of instructions, as they struggle to understand what is required of them (2.2.6–9). Second, although Cyrus' Persian friend Chrysantas has led the peers in agreeing to this change, a Persian captain, the 'rather austere' and 'most serious' (*spoudaiotaton*) Aglaitadas, objects to the levity of the anecdote and declines to believe that it is true (2.2.11, 16).[40] He tries to argue that lessons are better learned through weeping than through laughter, and that the joking stories are examples of charlatanry rather than wit.

After this exchange, Chrysantas notes that, as a consequence of the change in troop types, they must re-examine the equitable distribution of rewards and spoils; it would be wrong for rewards to be distributed equally among the expanded forces, when clearly some will contribute more than others. Xenophon nods again to Athens by having Cyrus propose a debate in the camp to decide the issue (2.2.18).[41] While his peers argue that Cyrus' decision should be final, Cyrus insists that the time is right (*kairos*) to discuss the matter openly, and the peers vote for the mass meeting. The two main speakers in the debate are Chrysantas for the peers and Pheraulas for the commoners. The latter, whom Xenophon describes as 'resembling a not ignoble man in body and soul', sums up the transition:

I recognize that we are all now beginning from the same place in our contest for excellence (*aretēs*). I see that we all exercise our bodies with the same nourishment, we are all considered worthy of being in the same company, and that the same goals lie in front of us all.   (*Cyr.* 2.3.8)

He goes on to suggest that skill in fighting with a sword and defending oneself in armed combat is natural (2.3.9–10); with the new training

---

[39] Arist. *Pol.* 4.6.1292b41–93a10, criticizing the volatility of law after the rise of the decree.
[40] I thank Luuk Huitink for discussion of this passage and its Platonic intertexts.
[41] Nadon 2001: 67–8, noting Aristotle's discussion (*Pol.* 3.9.1280a9–13).

regime, the commoners will quickly awaken latent skills, under the careful instruction of the peers and with a reward system instigated by Cyrus.[42]

Pheraulas, the virtuous commoner raised to great wealth through Cyrus' favour, appears again at the end of the work. When a Sacian, a warrior from the furthest region of Scythia, wins the horse race, he offers to exchange his horse with an honest man, and meets Pheraulas (*Cyr.* 8.3.25–32). The latter, unfulfilled by life in Cyrus' new regime, exchanges his new wealth and status with the outsider.[43]

A second change to the Persian forces restores the social hierarchy. Cyrus' time with his mother's family had given him the chance to learn to ride and develop skills in horsemanship, then largely unknown to the Persians, who did not keep horses (1.3.3). He proposes to his Persian peers that they also learn this skill and retrain as cavalry, to improve their capabilities in battle (4.3.3–23). But the change has implications for social status too, which would have been clear to Athenian readers. Now that all the commoners have become hoplites, the Persian elite can distinguish itself again by becoming cavalry, and in Athenian terms moving up in military and class status. Again, it is the Persian peer Chrysantas who expresses the benefits of the transition, in terms of ontological difference: mounted on horseback the Persian elite will become centaurs, or rather something better than a centaur, combining the best qualities of man and beast but capable of being separated (4.3.15–21).[44] Yet centaurs are semi-divine, and this transformation is suggestive of superiority. It restates the status divide between the elite and the commoners, undermined by Cyrus' retraining of the latter. Cyrus decrees that the elite should never be seen to go by foot, codifying the differentiation, and Xenophon notes this as a practice which continues to this day (*eti kai nun*, 4.3.23).

Spartan training: strengths and weaknesses

At its best, Spartan training delivered an unparalleled military machine. Xenophon's account of Agesilaus' provisions for training in his camps resembles his depiction of Cyrus' plans (*Cyr.* 2.2.6–9, and see above). He describes an ideal scene of careful preparation:

[42] Gray 2011b: 286; see also Plato's theory of recollection (*Meno*).
[43] Henderson 2012.
[44] Johnson 2005a.

As spring arrived, he gathered his whole army at Ephesus. Since he wanted it to train, he offered prizes for the cavalry companies, for whichever showed the best horsemanship, and for the hoplite companies, for whichever kept their bodies in the best condition. He also offered prizes for the companies of light-armed troops and archers, for whichever were best at the relevant skills. As a result, one could see the gymnasia full of men exercising, the horse-track of horses being trained, and spear-throwers and archers aiming at the target. Indeed he made the whole city in which they were camped worthy of seeing. For the marketplace was full of every kind of weapons and horses for sale, and the coppersmiths and carpenters and workers in iron and leather and painters were all making weapons of war; so that you might have thought that the city was a workshop of war (*polemou ergastērion*).   (*Agesilaus* 1.25–6)

This picture improves on the separate free and commercial marketplaces of Xenophon's Persia (*Cyr.* 1.2.3–4) by transforming commercial activity into preparation for war.

A belief in Sparta's superior capability on the battlefield was central to Athenian Laconophilia.[45] Xenophon appears to have assimilated his account of Persian training to his experience of Spartan training and the advantage that skill and practice conferred in combat. *The Constitution of the Spartans* asserts both the advantages of training on the field (*LP* 11.6–10) and also the requirement that Spartiates maintained their fitness while at home (12.5), although Xenophon does not go into details of Spartan training there.

The particular advantages that training conferred on the Spartans were resilience in formation and the ability to circle and re-form on the field, an ability Xenophon explores and idealizes in his battle narratives.[46] However, not all Spartan forces or leaders performed at the ideal level. Xenophon makes a negative exemplar of a campaign led by Mnasippus in 373 (*Hell.* 6.2.4–23).[47] After the Spartans suspected the Athenians of breaching a new peace treaty, they sent Mnasippus to guard the wealthy and strategically important island city of Corcyra. Mnasippus effectively besieged the *polis*, deploying well-located camps which cut the Corcyreans off from their farms, and preventing ships from reaching the port. However, his men, a mixture of Spartans and mercenaries, supplied themselves from the stores and cellars of wealthy Corcyrean estates, and lived luxuriously. When

---

[45] Ollier 1943.

[46] Konijnendijk 2018: 39–71 on the limits of training and Xenophon's emphasis on its necessity.

[47] Cawkwell 1979: 309 notes that Diodorus Siculus names other generals, suggesting that Mnasippus was not solely responsible for the campaign (DS 15.45.4, 15.46.2).

Corcyreans attempted to leave the city, Mnasippus whipped them and left them to die. His behaviour was reminiscent of the violence that Clearchus had demonstrated in the treatment of his own troops.[48] Lulled into a false sense of security by Corcyreans attempting to leave the city, Mnasippus stopped paying his mercenaries, and they left his service. Morale among the remaining Spartans was low, and not improved by Mnasippus beating a captain with a stick. The Corcyreans took advantage of the diminished Spartan strength and attacked his camp. Mnasippus did not have a large enough force to manoeuvre effectively on the battlefield, and was killed as the Spartans were defeated.

Xenophon contrasts Mnasippus with the Athenian general Iphicrates, who was sent out to rescue the Corcyreans. Iphicrates had recruited well for his campaign, equipped his fleet properly (*Hell.* 6.2.14), and trained his men well, making them row rather than rely on sail-power on their voyage around the Peloponnese, and even race each other (6.2.27–8), so that they arrived at full fitness and prepared to fight. En route he easily captured the Syracusan reinforcements sent to help Mnasippus' forces, and on arrival he took control of Corcyra. Xenophon praises both Iphicrates' military skill and the political acumen which led him to take political rivals on campaign with him (6.2.39). The unfortunate Mnasippus, in contrast, conformed to the stereotype of Spartan leadership that Xenophon established in his obituary of Clearchus.

Encountering other peoples

'On every page of the *Anabasis* the contrast between Greek and barbarian is sharply drawn', George Cawkwell noted.[49] Emily Baragwanath observes that it is 'a sustained reflection on the theme of Greeks in relation to barbarians'.[50] The Cyreans' encounters with different peoples add an ethnographic focus to the *Anabasis*.[51] Xenophon creates and explores oppositions between Greeks and Greeks from different communities, Persians, and non-Greek others such as the indigenous

---

[48] Hornblower 2000.
[49] Warner and Cawkwell 1972: 9.
[50] Baragwanath 2022: 131.
[51] Cf. Homer's *Odyssey*; Baragwanath 2022: 134; Lee 2008: 68–74.

peoples the Cyreans meet. Yet he also shows how a unified community can be constructed from diverse elements.

Xenophon sometimes gives differences between Greeks and others a moralizing tone, mapping them on to other oppositions. When Agesilaus campaigns in Persia, he orders that captured enemies (*barbarous*) be put up for sale naked, so that the sight of their soft white flesh would remind the Greek forces that they were fighting an enemy with feminine attributes (*Hell.* 3.4.19), lacking strength from a sedentary lifestyle. In the *Anabasis*, the enforcement of ethnic boundaries in the Greek camp marks a collective anxiety about the cohesion of the group. When one Apollonides disputes Xenophon's plans, his Boeotian accent does not prevent him from being identified as a non-Greek Lydian infiltrator and expelled (3.1.26–30).[52] But the episode may tell more of the strains of the construction of the community than of the lived experiences of actual individuals with complex intersecting identities at the margins of the Greek world.

The Ten Thousand's experience of the many different peoples they then encounter on their march is conditioned by adverse circumstances and their own aggression and defensiveness. They raid villages and farmland for provisions and plunder (*An.* 5.4.27, 5.5.6), and destroy communities, burning them down (5.2.27). It is hardly surprising that they encounter hostility. Xenophon critiques their behaviour as unjust and impious, arguing that the Greeks' mistreatment of the communities they pass through is counter-productive. The murder of the Cerasuntian ambassadors (5.7.19), for example, means that the Greeks will not be trusted and cannot expect hospitality or diplomacy in return for their wickedness (5.7.26–8). Subsequently, they encounter the Paphlagonians, poised between the Greek and barbarian worlds (6.1.26–8). This time, the Greeks receive the ambassadors correctly, entertaining them at a dinner which ends with displays of dancing; through his description, Xenophon shows the Paphlagonian bewilderment at the Greek dances in armour, and their shock at the stage-fighting and apparent wounding of a dancer. This reversal of perspective contrasts with the earlier depiction of the Mossynoecians as alien, from their obese and tattooed leaders to their taste for sex in public (5.4.30–4); their customs are opposite to those of the

---

[52] Huitink and Rood 2019: 90–1; Vlassopoulos 2013: 140–2.

Greeks.[53] The dance displays by different Greeks also emphasize the
Panhellenic make-up of the Cyreans.[54]

Conclusion

Xenophon's stories of campaigns and battles represent some of his
best-known writing. Because they are often shaped as exemplary
narratives, they have frustrated more recent historians seeking accurate
details of the events. But Xenophon's shaping of events shows how his
ideals for both leaders and their communities take shape in a military
context, supporting his repeated claim that leadership across home,
city, army, and empire is the same activity. By focusing on the details
which develop his analysis, he makes his case studies more effective.
These contain some of his most powerful and vivid writing, drawing
on his own experiences to formidable effect.

[53] Compare Herodotus' account of Egyptian customs; see Harrison 2003.
[54] Dillery 1995: 59.

VI. KINGDOM AND EMPIRE

Xenophon's thought on monarchy and the monarchical control of empire offers a distinctive contribution to political theorizing. He considers how an individual can be seen and agreed to merit the position of sole ruler, and so exercise power over his subjects identifies three main grounds for monarchical authority: ancestry, connection to the gods, and personal excellence (*Cyr.* 7.2.24). The phenomenon of royalty extends beyond the king himself, to his family and through his court. Royal women have a distinctive status compared with other women, with the possibility of greater agency. Xenophon depicts several such women, all from outside mainland Greece, as knowledgeable political actors and commentators: Mandane (*Cyr.* 1.3), Mania (*Hell.* 3.1.10–15), and Pantheia (*Cyr.* 4.6, 5.1, 6.1, 6.4, 7.3).[1]

Xenophon draws on earlier accounts, such as Herodotus' exploration of the role of kings in the rise and fall of the cities and empires they rule, and he parallels those of his contemporaries, notably Isocrates.[2] Their accounts of virtuous monarchical rule offer a different model from Plato's more abstract account (*Statesman, Euthydemus, Alcibiades I*). Xenophon's starting point is the Socratic idea of a 'kingly art' (*basilikē technē*), the skill of political leadership. He also borrows from the rich history of Achaemenid kingship, which drew on long traditions of wisdom literature and deployed the visual display of power and connection to the divine (*Anabasis, Cyropaedia, cf. Oeconomicus*).[3] This results in a conflict within Xenophon's monarchical thought, as the range of actions and strategies which he praises sit uncomfortably with conventional Greek views of virtue.[4]

Xenophon describes his ideal ruler most concisely in his portrait of Cyrus the Younger, not a king but pretender to the Achaemenid throne, in a brief obituary set within his account of Cyrus' fatal battle at Cunaxa (*An.* 1.9.1–29) and conveying the ambivalence some have seen in his account of the older Cyrus (*Cyropaedia*). The younger Cyrus was the 'most kingly (*basilikōtatos*) and most worthy of rule' of

---

[1] Emily Baragwanath has shown how Xenophon exploits the difference in lifestyle of Athenian women and non-Greek royal women: see Baragwanath 2002, 2016.

[2] See Atack 2020a: 122–50.

[3] Degen 2019; Tuplin 2013. Socrates' evocation of Persian kingship (Pl. *Alc.* 121b–122c) shows how Persian kings were productive examples for Greek thinkers.

[4] Although the schema in Buzzetti 2014 is too rigid; see Tamiolaki 2016b.

all the Persians after his older namesake (1.9.1). Even as a boy he had stood out from his peers for his heroic bravery in a hunting expedition – actions also suggesting a dangerous appetite for risk.[5]

Xenophon portrays Cyrus as concerned both with the maintenance of his reputation for honesty and with the need to outdo others when repaying favours or exacting punishment (1.9.10–11). His fierce punishments ensured public safety but left wrongdoers mutilated; at the same time, he was generous in rewarding the just, aiming to make 'the good more fortunate and the bad worthy of being their slaves' (1.9.15). His distribution of favours, from the food on his plate, to valuable gifts and land, was all aimed at securing his own pre-eminence, and made him 'loved by more people than any other Greek or barbarian' (1.9.29), the desired outcome of manipulative acts of generosity.[6] Despite his subservient status relative to his brother the king (Xenophon uses the word *doulou*, 'slave'), Persians became loyal to this junior figure rather than their Great King.[7]

The shepherd king and the metaphysics of monarchy

Since both Plato and Xenophon depict Socrates discussing *basilikē technē*, it seems likely that the concept was associated with the historical Socrates and his followers, as suggested by the discussion between Socrates and Aristippus (*Mem.* 2.1.17).[8] Other Socratics including Antisthenes wrote about kingship, and Antisthenes also used Cyrus as an exemplar (DL 6.16).[9] Perhaps paradoxically for thinkers focused on democratic Athens, the topic of kingship provided a structure for assessing both non-Greek regimes and political and military leadership more broadly.

Basilikē technē can imply a distinction between ruler and ruled, but the term is ambiguous. It denotes both a master skill, the 'king of skills' controlling all other skills, and the skill specific to ruling, the 'skill of kings'. For Dorion, the adjective 'kingly' should be seen primarily as

---

[5] Cf. *Cyr.* 1.4; Hom. *Od.* 19.428–66.
[6] Azoulay 2018a.
[7] On the terminology and its relation to Persian sources such as the Behistun inscription (DB 1), see Missiou 1993.
[8] See Chapter 4; Atack 2020a: 101–4.
[9] Antisthenes *SSR* V frs. 86, 97; Atack 2020a: 94–7; Prince 2015.

an analogy, in the first of these senses, and the skill should not be specifically associated with kings, the second sense.[10]

Both the Spartan and Persian systems of education taught this skill (see Chapter 4), as a means through which the endpoint of that education – the achievement of individual and collective happiness (*eudaimonia*) – might be reached. Xenophon suggests that what Socrates offered his students was the ability to lead as if they were a king. Socrates makes this explicit in his discussion with Euthydemus, identifying that he seeks:

the quality...which makes good politicians and good managers, men capable of exercising command and bringing benefit to people in general as well as themselves...This is the skill of kings, and we call it 'the royal art' (*basilikē technē*).   (*Mem.* 4.2.11)

This discussion does not confirm whether Socrates' *basilikē technē* is, paradoxically, a skill which might be best exercised in a *polis* setting over willing subjects, who can give and withhold consent. Xenophon argues that Cyrus had a unique capacity to engender willing submission to his rule and the desire to please him, but he exercises this beyond the scale of the *polis* (*Cyr.* 1.1.5).[11] Whether there can be room for a king in a *polis* citizen framework puzzled other theorists of Xenophon's time. Aristotle's account of kingship (*Politics* 3.14–18) concludes that a monarch (such as Xenophon's Cyrus) cannot be accommodated in the *polis*, because of his incommensurable excellence compared with other citizens who can never be his equals.[12] Where Xenophon treats the rule of the different entities of *polis* and empire as a transition of scale, Aristotle asserts a qualitative distinction between the *polis* and other types of community.

Xenophon's account of kingship incorporates the analogy between kings and shepherds common to both Greek and Near Eastern traditions. Homer's Agamemnon remains an important exemplar for Socrates, one who deserved the epithet 'shepherd of the people' (*Mem.* 3.2.1). This analogy invokes an image with significant cultural weight, much used by Homer (*Iliad* 2.243, 254) and with a long history in the ancient cultures of the Near East.[13] Xenophon's Cyrus develops

---

[10] Dorion 2004, 2013: 147–69; see also Illarraga 2023.

[11] Azoulay 2018a: 16; the reciprocal quality of *charis* is challenged in the context of monarchical superiority.

[12] David Riesbeck offers a different interpretation: see Riesbeck 2016: 258–69; Atack 2020a: 187–8.

[13] Brock 2013: 43–52; Haubold 2015; Atack 2020c.

the image through a consideration of the benefit that sheep and shepherd gain: profit for one, happiness (*eudaimonia*) for the other (*Cyr.* 8.2.14).[14]

In his *Statesman*, Plato appears to criticize the reactivation of this ancient image, through the extended myth of the Golden Age in which herds of humans are managed by semi-divine herders (Pl. *Plt.* 269c–275c).[15] His concern is the kind of difference implied between ruler and ruled; the shepherd-king image analogizes it to that between man and beast, or god and man.[16] Plato had previously suggested that a new form of difference might be found in the superior knowledge of the ideal rulers, the philosophers who should 'rule as kings' (*basileuein*) in an ideal city such as his posited Kallipolis (*Republic* 5.473d). Xenophon tends towards a weaker association between kings and the divine, crediting kings with special access to the gods and understanding of their intentions; this is in addition to holding formal religious roles such as priesthoods.

Xenophon's monarchical thought thus points to competing models of kings' authority, capturing a point of transition from what Alan Strathern labels the 'divinised king' to the 'righteous king'.[17] Strathern identifies a transformation of thought on kingship in what historians have termed the 'Axial Age'. The old idea that kings should rule because they had some measure of divinity, and were somehow aligned with the cosmos, or brought alignment with it, began to be replaced with a new sense that kings merited their rule through their personal qualities. Xenophon's and Plato's examination of the shepherd-king image suggests a recognition of that transition.

The *Cyropaedia*'s account of the Achaemenid kings explores their religious role (*Cyr.* 1.6.2–6, 8.3), suggesting a connection to the divine and ability to interpret it, rather than that kings are themselves divine.[18] In conversation with Cyrus, his father, Cambyses, responds to clear omens that Cyrus' expedition has the favour of the gods (1.6.1). He recalls how he has instructed Cyrus in the importance for a ruler of self-sufficiency in religious interpretation, 'so that you might not learn the advice of the gods from other people acting as interpreters, but you

---

[14] See Pl. *Rep.* 1.345c–e.
[15] See Atack 2020a: 154–58; on the *Statesman* myth, see Horn 2012.
[16] Cf. Arist. *Pol.* 1.2.1253a2–7.
[17] Strathern 2019: 155–218; Atack 2020a: 1–4. On the Axial Age, see Jaspers 1953.
[18] Melville and Mitchell 2013b; Root 1979, 2013.

would recognize it' (1.6.2). Cyrus' answers set out a pragmatic view of how leaders should manage their relationship with the gods. He notes that, in line with other relationships such as friendship, being properly prepared and having the skills to capitalize on circumstances is important for taking full advantage; in the case of the gods, this means paying due attention to them in both good times and bad (1.6.3), and being prepared to take advantage when the gods signal an opportunity (1.6.6). Cambyses' approach lies somewhere between grounding kingship in connection to the divine and in the possession of knowledge, illustrating the shifting grounds of political authority also explored by Plato (*Laws* 3.690a–c), in which authority based on knowledge is treated as the most developed form of authority, superseding patriarchal authority.

However, outside this dialogue, Xenophon hints at a strong sense of divine connection for Cyrus throughout the *Cyropaedia*. Before the vital battle against the Assyrians' allies, the Hyrcanians with their skilled cavalry, Cyrus prays for divine support, and one account (Xenophon signals authorial scepticism with *legetai*, 'it is said') describes Cyrus' forces being illuminated by divine light (*Cyr.* 4.2.15).[19] The mysterious light enables them to march through the night, and so surprise the Hyrcanians, resulting in the flight of the Assyrians from the field and a further victory for Cyrus.[20]

Other characters also assert the stronger view of the connection between Cyrus and the divine. When Cyrus captures Croesus, the defeated Lydian king suggests that the former possesses a fundamentally different form of monarchical authority:

I thought that I was capable of fighting against you, but first of all you are descended from the gods, and then from a line of kings, and finally you have been practising virtue from your childhood. But I understand that the first of my ancestors to rule as a king did so as one who was simultaneously king and freedman. (*Cyr.* 7.2.24)

Croesus accepts that Cyrus holds all three forms of monarchical authority – divinity, genealogy, and virtue – and acknowledges his innate superiority.[21] When Cyrus asks Croesus about his testing of oracles (a reference to Herodotus' longer account, Hdt. 1.46–56), the Lydian explains his own failings: that this exercise showed that he

[19] Gray 2011a.
[20] Degen 2019, 2020.
[21] Cf. Hdt. 1.6–7, and Xenophon's account of Agesilaus' claim to rule (*Ages.* 1.2).

misunderstood how to interact with the god Apollo. He still does not understand the answer which he received, Apollo's declaration that he will live in happiness through knowing himself (*Cyr.* 7.2.20).[22] Croesus' non-royal ancestry and failure to understand how to interact with the divine mark him as a failed king. But Xenophon's account of kingship encompasses different forms of successful kingship.

Two forms of kingship

Through his accounts of Cyrus the Great and Agesilaus, along with other kings, Xenophon creates two distinctive models of kingship. Sparta provides one form, a model of kingship which is clearly congruent with Xenophon's ethics of the self. The Spartan king Agesilaus II, in whose forces Xenophoon served in both Asia Minor and mainland Greece, provides an important example for his thought on monarchy. His depiction of Spartan kingship acknowledges the kings' traditional claims to authority but also shows how Agesilaus maintains and extends his authority through performance and ritual, in a process identified in Max Weber's account of charismatic leadership as 'routinization'.[23] This contrasts with the style of kings such as Astyages, and Cyrus in his imperial phase, in which authority is asserted performatively through differentiated appearance, and the display of wealth and power through court rituals and managed public appearances. While the first of these forms exemplifies a 'virtue' theory of monarchy shared by Xenophon's contemporary Isocrates (*Nicocles, Evagoras*), the second form conforms with it less obviously.[24]

The first form of kingship is associated with Sparta and the imagined Persia of the *Cyropaedia*. Spartan kingship rests on descent, religious role, and the exemplary virtue exhibited by kings such as Agesilaus. But it is a minimalist form of kingship compared with the second type, that of the *Cyropaedia*'s Medes and Xenophon's historical Persians. Its austerity appears more obviously congruent with Xenophon's Socratic ethics, and their emphasis on restraint and self-control. Other commentators thought it minimalist too: Aristotle, who appears to draw on the *Cyropaedia* at various points in his account

---

[22] Ellis 2016.
[23] See Atack 2023b.
[24] Atack 2018a.

of kingship, describes Spartan kingship as merely a combination of hereditary priesthood and generalship (*Pol.* 3.14.1285b26–8).

Xenophon sets out the privileges and duties of this kind of king in his *Constitution of the Lacedaimonians*. On campaign, the king performs sacrifices to the gods and gathers omens so that he can understand the will of the gods and decide whether any action should be taken, especially for symbolic actions such as crossing the border (*LP* 13.2–5). These are done in front of the commanders and two of the city's ephors.[25] When the Spartans march to battle, the king leads from the front. At home, the Lycurgan *politeia* prescribed a leading role for the king in religious matters, involving more public sacrifices (15.2), and also instituted a system for the king to dine in a public dining hall, where he had a double share of food so that he could make gifts of it to other diners (15.4). But mutual oaths between the kings and the ephors, as representatives of the city, commit the city's two kings to maintaining the existing *politeia* and not seeking to expand their power (15.7–8). Only on his death do the Spartans acknowledge that their king has a special status, treating him as a hero rather than a man (15.9). In this way, Xenophon argues, Spartan kingship avoids the risk of a king exceeding the limits of his authority and becoming a tyrant.

Xenophon's portrait of Agesilaus expands this description with telling details of how his claim to authority is made, drawn from his genealogical connection to the hero Heracles and, through him, the gods:

> About his noble ancestry (*eugeneias*) what might anyone say better or finer, than that even now (*eti kai nun*) they know how many generations of named ancestors he is from Heracles, and that these ancestors are not private individuals, but kings born from kings? (*Ages.* 1.2)

Agesilaus had secured his accession to the kingship because Spartans suspected the rival candidate, Leotychidas, of being fathered by the Athenian exile Alcibiades, a point which Xenophon leaves unexplained even as he emphasizes Agesilaus' legitimacy.[26]

Agesilaus demonstrates his connection to the past through the simplicity of his antique-looking home, which could even be the home of the first king (*Ages.* 8.7), and which demonstrates his restraint.[27]

---

[25] Humble 2022: 178–80.

[26] *Hell.* 3.3.1–4; *Ages.* 1.5; Plut. *Vit. Alc.* 23. Cartledge 1987: 112–14 notes discrepancies between Xenophon's two accounts.

[27] Compare stories of Romulus' hut from Rome: Dion. Hal. *Ant. Rom.* 1.79.11, Rood et al. 2020: 186–7.

Xenophon's Persian *politeia* does not mention the living arrangements for Cyrus' father, although it describes the king's military role (*Cyr.* 1.2.10). The Persian king's religious role becomes evident when Cyrus returns to Persia as supreme king over his father, Cambyses (8.5.22–6). The latter sets out the limits of Cyrus' role within Persia, which echo the limits of Spartan kingship.[28]

Spartan kingship offers a style of personal presentation which contrasts with that of non-royal leaders. Xenophon contrasts Agesilaus with the Spartan commander Lysander. The latter's extravagant personal presentation made him look more magnificent to the population of Asia Minor, attuned to the opulent display of Achaemenid power, so that they thought that 'Agesilaus appeared to be the private individual, and Lysander the king' (*Hell.* 3.4.7–8). However, Agesilaus responded by refusing all requests that Lysander brought to him, suggesting that his quietist mode of kingship did not indicate any abandonment of status hierarchies. Xenophon's insistence on the gulf between Lysander and the king marks his commitment to the idea that kingship is a form of leadership exercised on a different level. Xenophon later draws a related contrast, when Agesilaus meets the Persian king's local viceroy, the satrap Pharnabazus:

after agreeing a truce and shaking hands [Apollophanes] brought Pharnabazus to the specified place, where Agesilaus was lying on the ground on some grass waiting for him, with thirty of his associates. But Pharnabazus came wearing a robe worth much gold; and while his servants were laying out stitched blankets for him, on which the Persians sit in comfort (*malakōs*), he was ashamed to enjoy the luxury, as he saw the plain style of Agesilaus, so he too lay down on the ground just as he was.   (*Hell.* 4.1.30)

The contrast between the satrap, effectively a royal figure, and the Spartan king illuminates the contrast between the two forms of kingship in Xenophon's work, which is more broadly explored in the *Cyropaedia*. Here the distinction between the forms of kingship is coded into Greek-like and non-Greek forms.[29] While Cyrus' Persian father, Cambyses, represents a style of kingship resembling the Spartan form, his Median maternal grandfather, Astyages, exemplifies a maximalist form of monarchical performance, exhibiting all the features

---

[28] Atack 2023a; Tuplin 1994.
[29] On the Greek 'despotic template', see Dewald 2003; on Xenophon's presentation of Achaemenid courts, see Tuplin 2010.

of a palace system in which the king occupies a special place of
extreme privilege and displays high levels of consumption and display,
emphasizing the gap between ruler and ruled. The young Cyrus
criticizes this distinction when he returns to Persia, arguing that kings
should be distinguished by their commitment to effort:

> they consider it necessary that the ruler should differ from the ruled in dining more
> sumptuously and having more money in his store and sleeping for longer and leading
> a life more lacking in toil (aponōteron) than that of the ruled. But I think that the ruler
> should not differ in his use of leisure time but in thinking ahead and loving hard work
> (philoponein). (Cyr. 1.6.8)

Xenophon presents Astyages' court as a site of an exoticized despotic rule
in which the elite enjoy a luxurious life and are visibly distinguished from
those they rule. Cyrus noticed his grandfather's royal costume and self-
presentation, the eye make-up, rouge, and wig (Cyr. 1.3.2); although
his initial response was negative, he would later adopt it himself as a
marker of his new kingly status (Cyr. 7.5.37).[30] Here Xenophon transforms aspects of the despotic template into an account of effective governance; the second form of kingship can also be a form of virtue monarchy.

Cyrus' actions and habits secure good behaviour from his subordinates
by providing an example (paradeigma) for them to imitate (8.1.37):

> We agree that we have learned of Cyrus that he considered that rulers should not differ
> from their subjects in this way alone, through being better than them, but he also
> thought that they should also use enchantment (katagoēteuein). At any rate, he himself
> chose to wear Median dress, and he persuaded his colleagues (koinōnas) to dress
> themselves in it. For it seemed to him to cover up if anyone had any deficiencies
> in their body, and to make its wearers look most handsome and of greatest stature (kal-
> listous kai megistous). (Cyr. 8.1.40)

The make-up and costume which the young Cyrus had disdained now
appear useful to him as a way of signalling status and exerting authority
which can be communicated through others, so that his personal
charisma can be spread to a greater distance. Xenophon concludes
that his stylized appearance on formal occasions constitutes one of the
'arts he devised so that his rule might appear difficult to despise (mē
eukataphronēton)' (8.3.1). He goes on to describe Cyrus' preparations
for a key religious procession, in which he puts on magnificent robes,
and gives matching ones, minus the purple stripes denoting royalty,

---

[30] Tatum 1989: 97–111; Azoulay 2004; Atack 2018a.

to his associates (8.3.13–14). The spectacle is such that even Cyrus' close associates respond by performing *proskynēsis*, a gesture of obeisance, contrary to their own customs.[31]

One way in which Cyrus exerts his power remotely is through transmitting his excellence to his subordinates, while at the same time exercising power through the manipulation of his appearance and public image. The king demonstrates his authority by providing a model of behaviour to copy, directly to his courtiers. Xenophon presents both Cyrus and Agesilaus as exemplars or *paradeigmata* for imitation. Being an exemplar makes demands on the ruler; these extend from principles of military leadership, as Cyrus and Cambyses discuss. The leader must be prepared to undergo hardship and to show more physical resilience than those he leads (1.6.24–6, cf. 1.6.8). As they note, the potential rewards for success and penalties for failure are also greater for leaders, because their exposed position makes dishonour all the greater.

Cyrus, after he has assumed full power, insists that both he and his immediate deputies must demonstrate the excellence which underpins their claim to that power. While the favour of the gods will help them, they must also help themselves:

After this, the most powerful [support] we must provide for ourselves. This is being considered worthy of ruling through being better than those who are ruled. Therefore we must share hot and cold and food and drink and labour and rest even with our slaves. But while we share in these experiences with them we must try to show that we are better than them.   (*Cyr.* 7.5.78)

However, what Cyrus insists must not be shared is the 'theoretical and practical knowledge of war' (*polemikēs epistēmēs kai meletēs*, 7.5.79), which is instrumental in the elite's pursuit of freedom and happiness. The performative display of resilience and endurance is not an invitation to their inferiors to copy and learn; the only ones for whom the austere leaders are exemplars (*paradeigmata*) are their sons.

That Xenophon believes that both forms of kingship can deliver excellence is shown in the similar qualities he assigns to Agesilaus and Cyrus.[32] In the *Agesilaus*, he devotes separate chapters to each aspect of virtue which Agesilaus exemplifies: piety (3.1), honesty

[31] Bowden 2013.
[32] Azoulay 2020.

(4.1), self-restraint in pursuing his sexual desires (5.1), courage (6.1), love of country (7.1), and charm, his ability to deploy *charis* (8.1).

The construction of exemplary narratives is sometimes at odds with telling the historical truth. Because Xenophon includes Agesilaus' military campaigns in both his *Hellenica* and his flattering biographical portrait, *Agesilaus*, it is possible to see him moulding his material to produce a more compelling exemplar. Accounts of Cyrus from other sources – Herodotus and Ctesias – suggest similar operations in Xenophon's construction of the *Cyropaedia*.[33] While Herodotus depicted Cyrus dying in a conflict with the Massagetae after proposing marriage to their queen (Hdt. 1.205–14), Xenophon depicts him dying peacefully in old age (*Cyr.* 8.7.2–28). Both accounts feature warning dreams sent by the gods, but only in Xenophon's version is Cyrus able to advise his sons.

When Cyrus completes his conquest of surrounding lands with his victory at Babylon, he transforms himself from the leader of an army to the ruler of an empire, as he enters the city. Along with the decision to treat the conquered as subjected peoples, he makes a conscious decision to present himself in the style of the Medes rather than the Persians:

> He commanded the Babylonians to work their lands and to pay tribute and to serve (*therapeuein*) those to whom each of them had been allotted; he told the Persians who were his partners (*koinōnous*) and those of the allies who chose to stay with him to speak as masters (*despotas*) to those whom they had captured.
>
> After this, although Cyrus already desired to set himself up as he thought appropriate for a king, he thought he should do this with the agreement of his friends; that he should appear infrequently and in solemnity in a way which attracted the least jealousy.
>
> (*Cyr.* 7.5.36–7)

In choosing to limit his contact with others, Cyrus adopts the seclusion which for Greeks marks the oriental despot.[34] Cyrus expresses this model when he sets up his palace system and transforms the status of his associates, who take on new roles as courtiers and key subordinates, and so retain some access to him. The vast scale of the royal household established by Cyrus in Babylon echoes other descriptions of palace systems, such as Herodotus' account of the Median king Deioces' palace at Ecbatana (Hdt. 1.98–100). Xenophon describes the palace

---

[33] Lenfant 2004; Gray 2016. On the historical Cyrus, see Briant 2002; Mitchell 2023.
[34] On Xenophon and Persian culture, see Hirsch 1985.

system in detail, but the account functions as a normative model. Notable are Cyrus' meticulous plans for the protection of his person, with carefully selected eunuchs as his personal bodyguard, and with an outer layer of protection from an elite force of troops, the Ten Thousand (*Cyr.* 7.5.58–68). Again, there is a rationale: eunuchs have no family loyalties so rely entirely on patronage, while his elite force are hand-picked from the poor Persians who would easily be bound in the same way.

Kingship between virtue and vice

The encounters between Cyrus and Croesus and Agesilaus and Lysander assert a difference between kings and other leaders. Although Xenophon occasionally declares the similarity of leadership over different domains, from empire to household, his kings display differences, from their superior epistemic status to their ability to deploy that status to dominate and manipulate subjects through ruses and deception. These powers lead to what some have labelled 'dark' readings of the *Cyropaedia* as a manual for tyranny rather than virtuous rule.[35] Xenophon's description of Cyrus' imperial regime contains some of his most detailed political thinking, albeit targeted to a mode of rule and social organization antithetical to the democratic *polis*. Cyrus' control over his people, from the crowds who line Babylon's streets for processions to the distant subjects who cannot expect to see him, is maintained by institutions which focus power on him while enabling that power to be distributed and delegated.

As Vincent Azoulay showed, Cyrus weaponizes the concept of *charis*, the tradition of reciprocal generosity between friends and fellow citizens.[36] He donates huge rewards to his closest associates, giving them provinces to rule as well as great riches and rewards, but they cannot hope to reciprocate and so remain under obligation to him. They must be present at court to display their loyalty (*Cyr.* 8.1.16–21), and are punished for failure to attend. Rodrigo Illarraga has demonstrated a structure to Xenophon's account which balances the contributions of Cyrus' psychology and his education, answering the

---

[35] Gray 2011b.
[36] Azoulay 2018a.

question posed in the opening chapter, so that Cyrus' pursuit of honour (*philotimia*) is aimed at virtuous ends.[37]

While written law still has a role in Cyrus' regime, the power of the ruler plays a greater part in ensuring conformity: 'Cyrus considered that a good ruler over men is a seeing law (*bleponta nomon*), because he is capable of setting them in order, and seeing and punishing the disorderly' (*Cyr.* 8.1.14). Cyrus can engage in remote perception of his subjects through his structures of command and control. These include motivating some subjects to act as 'the king's eyes' and 'the king's ears' in return for generous rewards (8.2.10–12). As Xenophon explains, this is not a role held by a specific individual, but a practice in which all may engage, and which ensures continuous conformity.[38] But this system is only part of a hierarchy through which power is transmitted downwards and across Cyrus' vast empire.

The special epistemic status of the king permits him to deploy strategies not available to others, in withholding and obscuring knowledge from both his enemies and his subjects. Xenophon's royal characters appear to accept that there are circumstances in which they should use tactics similar to Plato's 'noble lie' (Pl. *Rep.* 3.414b–417b), deceiving others to benefit them.[39] War is agreed to be such an occasion, but the *Cyropaedia* explores the role of deception in leadership, giving rise to further questions: whether Xenophon regards Cyrus as an ideal or not, and whether his regime should be admired. In 'republic to empire' readings, Cyrus' use of deception is treated as a negative quality. Joseph Reisert characterizes Cyrus as 'a sort of moral black hole around which the whole galaxy of his subordinates and subjects will come to revolve'.[40] These responses sometimes draw on Straussian arguments, in which Xenophon's apparent praise of Cyrus conceals a sharp critique.[41]

In a key discussion early in the *Cyropaedia*, Cambyses discuss the roles of truth and deception in leadership with his son as the latter leaves Persia to begin his campaign. After a long and wide-ranging discussion on the importance for leaders of being knowledgeable and able to command respect and obedience, of leading by example, and

---

[37] Illarraga 2021.
[38] Azoulay 2018a
[39] Hesk 2000: 151–62; Schofield 2007, 2023: 139–62.
[40] Reisert 2009: 302; see also Newell 1983; Nadon 2001.
[41] Tamiolaki 2020b.

demonstrating a greater capacity for enduring the hardships required
on campaign, Cyrus asks how to gain advantage over the enemy
(*Cyr.* 1.6.19–26). Cambyses begins by setting out the moral complexity
of leadership, such that a leader may sometimes use questionable tactics to achieve an acceptable goal:

> Be aware that the man who is going to do these things must be a plotter and secretive
> and a trickster and deceptive, a thief and a bandit, making gains from the enemy in
> every act...if you were that kind of man, my son, you would be a man with the greatest
> respect for justice and the law.   (*Cyr.* 1.6.27)

Cambyses goes on to explain that many of the skills that the Persian
boys learn have bad as well as good uses, such as the tricks used to
trap prey on hunting expeditions (1.6.28). Young boys use trickery
only against animals, and are taught 'to tell the truth, not to trick
and not to take advantage' (1.6.33), a practice which the Persians
enacted as law in response to the Greek fashion for teaching deception
(1.6.31–2), and also perhaps a criticism of Spartan practices.[42] This
creates the counter-intuitive point that the ideal leader, the paradigm
of virtue, is able to use non-virtuous forms of persuasion, rhetorical
strategies such as deception and theft which are forbidden to the
subjects, to encourage them to obey. This disjunction opens up the
possibility of readings in which Xenophon's text, like the actions it
describes, offers the elite a lesson inaccessible to those whom they
lead.[43] Others, such as Christopher Nadon, focus on the implications
for the regime Cyrus institutes after his conquests are complete; this
'republic to empire' reading of the *Cyropaedia* follows Machiavelli's
analysis of the role of deception in the exercise of power, and questions
whether any 'straightforward' reading of the work is possible.[44]

   While these readings emphasize moments of ambivalence and
complexity in Xenophon's portrait of Cyrus, they underplay the
importance of the many Greek antecedents for the use of trickery by
leaders. Odysseus is a prime example of a trickster leader, exemplifying
the quality of *mētis*, a cunning intelligence which is praiseworthy in a
military or political leader.[45] It also downplays Xenophon's clear rejection

---

[42] Hesk 2000: 122–41. See also Chapter 4.
[43] See Newell 1983. On Xenophon, Machiavelli, and deception, see Rasmussen 2009 for a
Straussian-tinged analysis.
[44] Nadon 1996, 2001: 1–13, criticizing the literary readings of Due 1989 and Gera 1993 among
others.
[45] Detienne and Vernant 1974; Odysseus is the paradigmatic example of *mētis* in leadership.

of another form of deception, the over-promising of benefits. A leader's credibility and authority will evaporate quickly if he raises expectations and fails to deliver (1.6.19), and no-one will be willing to follow him; this form of dishonesty is not acceptable, whether one is leading a pack of hounds or a band of soldiers. Likewise, people are willing to obey those who seem skilled and to be acting with goodwill and concern for their interests.

Cyrus does not rely on *mētis* at the start of his development as a leader. He first deploys it as he overtakes his uncle Cyaxares as effective leader of the Median forces (*Cyr.* 4.2). Cyrus has been keen to follow up their battlefield action with pursuit of their opponents, but Cyaxares declines to send out a raiding party, preferring to spend the evening hosting a feast for his commanders. Cyrus asks for permission to take volunteers on a raid, seizes the opportunity, and, as Xenophon takes great pains to show, seeks the support of the gods in doing so (4.2.12). While the gods send a divine light to illuminate his journey (4.2.15; see p. 109 above), and enable him to return victorious with further spoils, Cyaxares becomes resentful of his nephew's activity.

Xenophon uses this episode to show that Cyrus' skill and qualities play an important part in his success. Another element of Xenophon's conception of leadership, the ability of leaders to recognize moments of opportunity, originates from a military context: the word *kairos* is often used by historians to denote the good order of forces readied for battle.[46] But Cyrus' ability to recognize the opportune moment and act on it is recognized by the steady drift of allied troops to his command. The arrival of a large Persian force after the battle is over cements his rise in status.

Cyaxares' complaint to Cyrus and their subsequent discussion provide a second dialogue on the nature of monarchy (5.5). Cyaxares recognizes that he is diminished by Cyrus' success and the material evidence for it. Although he is 'born from a king and from ancient ancestry which reaches back as far as human memory, and considered a king himself', he sees that he is visibly less successful and has a lesser entourage than Cyrus (5.5.8).

Cyaxares' complaint is that Cyrus' energy and successful action have alienated his own support and dishonoured him (5.5.25–6). He illustrates the way Cyrus has won the support of the Medes using

---

[46] Trédé 1992; Atack 2018b connects this to the account of the *kairos* in Plato's *Statesman*.

two examples: petting another man's hunting dogs (5.5.28) and seducing his wife (5.5.30).[47] Cyaxares feels emasculated by Cyrus' success, claiming that he has been excluded from sharing in honourable activity and instead receiving favours 'like a woman', while Cyrus performs the masculine role (5.5.33). This is one of many examples of Xenophon analogizing monarchical power to the patriarchal power of a man over his wife and household.

Monarchy and gender

Kings occupy the top place in any non-divine hierarchy. In doing so, they display a hyper-masculinity which emasculates those they dominate, as Xenophon makes explicit in his account of Cyrus' encounters with Cyaxares and Croesus. Royal performance transcends gender norms: Cyrus' adoption of facial make-up represents both royal seclusion – people cannot see his true face – and a way of signalling his power, rather than the negative assessment of women's use of make-up seen in the *Oeconomicus*.

Royal women also transcend gender norms through their proximity to power. Cyrus rewards the masculine-coded courage of the Armenian prince Tigranes' wife with a gift of 'feminine jewellery' (*gynaikeion kosmon*, *Cyr.* 8.4.24). Women can participate more directly in palace-based monarchical regimes than in the *polis*; the palace is effectively a large household, and they also accompany their husbands on campaign. This gives women like Tigranes' wife and Pantheia opportunities for action. Just as Ischomachus' wife exercises knowledge in managing their household and discusses and criticizes her husband's actions, royal women display knowledge in administering the palace, negotiating its hierarchies, and assessing the performance of their male kin.[48]

Cyrus' mother, Mandane, voices the clearest assessment of the risk of tyranny and the impact of tyranny on community (1.3.13–18). She has taken her son to visit her father, Astyages, the king of the Medes, where he has experienced its palace culture and the unlimited power wielded by his grandfather. She is concerned that this experience will undermine his commitment to Persian republican values. While Cyrus is

---

[47] Cf. Croesus at *Cyr.* 7.2.28–9.
[48] Baragwanath 2002.

confident that he will retain his earlier lessons in justice from Persia, Mandane sets out the difference between the two forms of kingship clearly:

> 'But, my son,' she said, 'at your grandfather's court and in Persia the same things are not agreed to be just (*dikaia*). For he has made himself the master (*despotēn*) of everyone in Media, while in Persia having an equal share (*to ison echein*) is considered just. But your father is first to do what is ordered by the city, and he accepts those orders, and the measure is not his soul (*psuchē*) but the law (*nomos*).' (*Cyr.* 1.3.18)

Mandane's clearsighted political analysis reflects a broader trend in Greek historiography; Herodotus, too, depicts the women of royal households as perceptive analysts of politics and religion.[49] Because women moved from one household to another on marriage, Mandane's life has given her experience of two cultures and a comparative perspective. Xenophon uses her to explore the possibility of a hybridization of his two forms of kingship through uniting the differentiated cultures of Medes and Persians.

The Asian queen Pantheia, 'the most beautiful woman', plays a significant role in the *Cyropaedia*. Her story explores key ethical themes while being interwoven with that of Cyrus; it appears to some as a romantic sub-plot, but in exploring both self-control (*enkrateia*) and the limits of *charis* it provides an opportunity for Xenophon to explore key ethical themes.[50] Pantheia enters the story when she is captured as Cyrus' forces defeat the Assyrian forces with which her husband, Abradatas, king of Susa, is allied. Distributing the human spoils of war is complicated; Cyrus decides to keep her as a hostage rather than to enslave her (5.1.17, 6.4.7). Cyrus' friend Araspas reports her incredible beauty, which leads Cyrus to decline to meet her lest he be distracted from his mission (5.1.8).[51]

Cyrus places Pantheia in the care of Araspas, expecting that she will become useful in some way (5.1.17). However, although Araspas has sworn that he will maintain self-control and not mistreat her, he lacks Cyrus' self-control, becomes obsessed with his beautiful charge, and, when she rejects his approaches, threatens her. Pantheia does not submit to his harassment, but sends one of her eunuch retinue to

---

[49] E.g. Gorgo at Hdt. 5.51; cf. Tomyris, queen of the Massagetae, Hdt. 1.212–15.

[50] The episode has a rich bibliography: Due 1989: 79–83; Gera 1993: 221–45; Tatum 1989: 163–88; Stadter 1991: 480–4; Whitmarsh 2018: 60–2.

[51] See Chapter 2.

demand action from Cyrus (6.1.31–3). Cyrus' resolution of the incident demonstrates how he gains considerable advantage from those around him. After he removes her from Araspas' control, the grateful Pantheia offers Cyrus the support of her husband (6.1.38–40). She commissions new armour for her husband, made from her jewellery, and sends him to fight for Cyrus in a vivid and touching scene which emphasizes Cyrus' status as a heroic figure and *kalos kagathos* (6.4.2–11).

Cyrus finally meets and sees Pantheia as she mourns over the mutilated corpse of Abradatas, retrieved from the battlefield (7.3.8–12). While he offers continuing protection for her, she blames both herself and Cyrus for her husband's death. Pantheia is one of very few characters whom Xenophon depicts criticizing Cyrus, and perhaps the most justified. After Cyrus leaves, she takes her own life (7.3.14).

In lower levels of Persian imperial administration, Xenophon shows how an exceptional woman can operate as a leader. After the death of her husband Zenis, Mania asks the satrap Pharnabazus to be allowed to take over his role as governor of Aeolis (*Hell.* 3.1.10–12).[52] She performs well, keeping the area loyal, supporting Pharnabazus' raids on the neighbouring peoples, and offering the satrap appropriate hospitality. However, as the years pass, her son-in-law finds it intolerable to be governed by a woman; because she did not guard against her own family, he is able to assassinate her and her son (3.1.14). The story of Mania echoes Herodotus' tales of women as leaders, but it also illustrates the precarity of their power.

Tyranny and autocracy

Not all single-person rule is good; theoretical idealism gives way to the knowledge of lived reality. The encounter between two non-Greek sole rulers, Cyrus and Croesus, shows that there are different forms of monarchical power (*Cyr.* 7.2), with the case for the difference being made by the defeated Croesus. And in the short dialogue *Hiero*, Xenophon examines the rule of an extra-constitutional Greek sole ruler exerting power as his only means of authority. In both these conversations, Xenophon engages broadly with the literary topos of the encounter between the wise man and the tyrant; both also critique earlier examples of the genre, especially Herodotus' accounts of the

[52] Azoulay 2007; Baragwanath 2016.

meetings of Solon and Croesus (Hdt. 1.29–33) and of Cyrus with Croesus (Hdt. 1.86–91).[53]

Tyranny is a deprecated form of rule, the 'bad' form of monarchy in the sixfold typology of constitutions (*Mem.* 4.6.12). In tyrannies, an individual holds political power without any authority beyond their own coercive power, and dominates the community without the consent of the ruled. Tyranny lacks the cosmic and divine authority of kingship, a point noted by Croesus, the *turannos* of Lydia, as he compares his own rule of the Lydians with that of Cyrus (*Cyr.* 7.2.21–4).[54] While Croesus has amassed great wealth, he lacks understanding of the divine, and has misinterpreted a key message from Delphi; even the idea of testing oracles is somewhat impious (see pp. 109–10 above). Croesus finally achieves understanding in the recognition that, after his defeat has emasculated him, he will have a happy life enjoying his wealth with no continuing responsibility (7.2.27–8), living a life that parallels the one that his wife enjoyed during his successful years.

Croesus' assessment of his changed situation offers a novel answer to the question of tyranny and happiness, placing it within Xenophon's overarching conceptual framework, within which all forms of organization can be analogized to the household. There was a popular view that an individual with unrestricted power and the capacity to satisfy all their desires must, from a hedonist perspective, be the happiest of all men, and his condition must be a desirable one.[55]

Xenophon also critically examines this topos in the *Hiero*, which features two historical fifth-century people apparently in the role of ruler and adviser: Hieron, the tyrant of Syracuse, and the poet Simonides, who was famous for writing praise poems to order, often for tyrannical leaders.[56] While Xenophon draws on the historical situation of both his characters, they also both inhabit and subvert the stock types of tyrant and wise adviser. As with the *Cyropaedia*, the *Hiero* has attracted divergent interpretations. Vivienne Gray follows other scholars who have accepted that Xenophon is straightforwardly suggesting, through Simonides in the role of adviser, a way in which a tyrant can transform

---

[53] Gray 1986.

[54] The term *turannos* may originate in a Lydian context, where it denotes a legitimate hereditary ruler, albeit one whose dynastic line came to power by force (V. Parker 1998).

[55] Pl. *Grg.* 470d–471d, where Polus claims this status for the Macedonian king Archelaus; see also McGlew 1993: 32–3.

[56] Strauss argues that Simonides, as a Socratic figure, conceals his wisdom in the dialogue (L. Strauss 2013: 38–40); cf. Zuolo 2017; Dorion and Bandini 2021.

himself into a king, and simultaneously legitimize his power and bring happiness to those he rules.[57] She argues that the suggestions Simonides makes could transform Hieron from tyrant to something resembling Aristotle's *pambasileus*.[58] Others have been less sure, finding complex irony in the work, both in Hieron's developing presentation of his plight (*Hiero* 2–8) and in Simonides' response and advice (9–11).[59] Claudia Mársico has pointed to connections with the discussion of tyranny in Platonic texts, although, unusually, in this case the *Alcibiades* and *Hipparchus* may be pseudepigraphic additions to the corpus and so post-date Xenophon's thought on the topic; there are also parallels in the account of tyranny in *Republic* 9.[60]

Still other commentators have pointed to Plato's critical use of Simonides as a character to represent past forms of knowledge which are now obsolescent: his definition of justice is rejected at the outset of the *Republic* (1.331d–334e), and a significant section of the *Protagoras* (338e–347a) is devoted to a detailed critique of the maxims embedded in one of his poems.[61] This critique fits within a broader fourth-century challenge to the literary and cultural authority of the poets (Isoc. *Evagoras* 8–11), which makes it harder to read Xenophon's portrayal of Simonides as uncomplicatedly positive.[62]

Simonides asks Hieron of Syracuse to instruct him in how the life of a tyrant differs from that of an ordinary citizen (*Hiero* 1.1–2). Hieron is a tyrant in the normal Greek usage of the term, an extra-constitutional ruler of a *polis* whose rule depends on the exercise of power. Simonides expects an answer which presents the 'happy tyrant' model, but Hieron gives him the opposite, arguing that the apparent oppressor is in fact the oppressed. The tyrant, who has no apparent constraint on his resources or actions, and so is popularly supposed to be able to maximize his pleasure and be happy, is paradoxically more constrained than the private individuals he dominates, and less happy, because of his fear of those he dominates attacking him. The private citizen therefore has more freedom than the ruler, and more capacity to satisfy sensory desires: for example, private individuals can travel to attend festivals

---

[57] Gray 2007: 34.
[58] Arist. *Pol.* 3.16–17; Gray 2007: 30.
[59] E.g. Too 2021: 119–30, who suggests that the didactic authority of poetry is also under question.
[60] Mársico 2023.
[61] McCoy 1999.
[62] Dorion and Bandini 2021: cxlix–clxxvii.

and events, while the tyrant is afraid to leave his secure base at home for insecure venues (1.12).[63]

Hieron gives multiple examples to support his claim that he cannot experience happiness, in response to Simonides' questions. The tyrant has no meaningful relationships in which to take pleasure: he must always assume that any praise is flattery, and that any lover who accepts his advances does so out of fear rather than willingly. Because all his wishes are easily fulfilled, he cannot take pleasure in anticipating the future fulfilment of his desires. The normal human connections between family and friends (*philia*) are impossible under the conditions of tyranny; family and friends are often those who assassinate tyrants (3.6–8). Lovers offer only flattery, not any sense of a genuine interpersonal connection.

In the second half of the dialogue (8–11), Simonides changes his tactics and offers suggestions for how Hieron might become more fulfilled and alleviate his fear of his subjects by transforming the way in which he rules. On a positive reading of the dialogue, this advice would enable the tyrant to transform himself into a king, by legitimizing his rule. If Hieron were to gain the trust of those he oppresses, by demonstrating goodwill towards them and pursuing goals which benefited the community, he could win their assent to his rule and so relieve himself of fear. Simonides' suggestions have a strongly Xenophontic ring to them, as much as a Socratic one.[64] He suggests organizing the citizens into tribes and instituting competitions between them, for military training and business expertise (9.6), agricultural productivity (9.7), and entrepreneurship (9.9–10). The prizes which Hieron provides will encourage citizens to invest in the hope of securing victory, as those funding Athenian tragedies did (9.4–6). Whether such competition represents aristocratic agonism or market forces, Simonides' suggestions are appropriate both to his context, as a writer of victory odes, and to Xenophon's practice. Cyrus, for example, instituted competitions among his troops to encourage them to train (*Cyr.* 1.6.18, 2.1.22–3; see Chapter 5).

Simonides suggests that Hieron keep his mercenaries but use them to protect the whole community, rather than protecting him from that community (*Hiero* 10.1–8). Hieron should further invest in the city, competing with other rulers in the adornment of his community.

---

[63] The historical Hieron's teams competed and won at major festivals.
[64] Dorion and Bandini 2021: lxiii–lxviii.

This will cause the citizens to love him; he will be overwhelmed with their erotic desire (11.11). As Victoria Wohl notes, Xenophon's language here evokes a democratic topos of erotic love between citizen and city.[65] Historical tyrants, notably Athens' Peisistratids, had acted as benefactors to the city, and had driven many cultural developments which took full form under the democracy.[66]

Xenophon's accounts of Hieron and Croesus both emphasize personal relationships and explore how power transforms and corrupts them. His closing chapter in the *Cyropaedia* suggests that the Achaemenid dynasty is similarly corrupted by its power, with king and court failing to follow the precepts given by Cyrus to maintain the skills and habits developed in the austere Persian tradition (*Cyr.* 8.8.4–7).

Hegemony in the Greek world as monarchical power

Although the Greek world of Xenophon's time was made up of multiple independent cities with varied political regimes, larger and more powerful cities, such as Athens and Syracuse, exerted power over smaller ones, especially those of strategic importance for trade and resources. Such rule could be characterized as a form of monarchical rule. Thucydides' history had noted the difficulties of maintaining such rule, in Pericles' 'policy' speech (Thuc. 2.59–64), and in the 'Melian Dialogue' had made implicit criticism of the Athenian ideology which had supported imperialism (5.84–116). Xenophon had seen both Athens lose its 'empire' of Greek cities around the Aegean, originally its allies in the Delian League against a notional Persian threat, during the Peloponnesian War, and also its attempt to reassert its hegemonic status after the failure of Spartan leadership. His military experience coincided with the period in which Sparta had become the hegemonic power of the Greek world. The later parts of the *Hellenica* explore the collective failings of leadership exhibited by Sparta.[67] The strife for leadership among the Greek forces of the *Anabasis* also reflects these inter-*polis* disputes. Xenophon is severely critical of Spartan leadership in both works.

[65] Wohl 2002: 241–4.
[66] Zatta 2009.
[67] Tuplin 1993.

Near contemporaries of Xenophon, such as Isocrates, argued for a new Panhellenic alliance and expedition against Persia, ideally led by Athens, as a response to the changing international situation in the first half of the fourth century.[68] Xenophon is explicit in articulating similar Panhellenic goals; he envisages the Cyreans returning to Asia Minor after they have reached Greece, in order to exploit its wealth (*An.* 3.2.24–6).[69] As John Dillery argues, both Cyrus' own assessment of the Greeks and also their later success in finding their way home display Persia as weak compared with Greek capabilities.[70] The fertility and wealth of the lands ruled by the Great King offered a tempting alternative to the real and increasing poverty of Athens. Agesilaus' campaign is cast in Panhellenic terms, introduced by Xenophon as such (*Hell.* 3.1.1–2); in the *Agesilaus*, he praises the king's plans for revenge on Persia (*Ages.* 1.8).[71] But the Cyreans did not return to Greece, and Agesilaus' campaign in Asia ended without a significant outcome; the king returned to Sparta when summoned by the ephors (*Ages.* 1.36–8). Xenophon shows the constitutionally limited king recognizing the limits of the Panhellenic dream. Chapter 5 of the *Poroi* suggests an ambivalent attitude to military adventures in any recovered Athenian hegemony.[72]

Conclusion

Xenophon's thoughts on monarchy are some of his most interesting and, as the concluding chapter shows, most influential in later antiquity and up to early modern times. His accounts of figures such as Cyrus and Agesilaus enable him to explore different modes of kingship and to incorporate the performative elements he felt central to Achaemenid kingship into his model of good leadership. But these accounts also enable him to explore ethical topics, and how and even whether a good life can be lived in conditions of extreme abundance or absolute power. The *Cyropaedia* and the *Hiero* both provide important expansions of his ethical thought.

---

[68] See Low 2018.
[69] Warner and Cawkwell 1972: 23–4.
[70] Dillery 1995: 60.
[71] Dillery 1995: 99–101.
[72] Farrell 2016.

VII. CONCLUSION: XENOPHON THROUGH TIME

As Chapter 2 noted, the critical evaluation of Xenophon by scholars has changed over time. Nineteenth- and twentieth-century criticisms of his philosophical and historical writing have now largely been replaced by an appreciation of both the literary qualities of his work and the evidence they provide for the thought of his time, as well as his own contribution. While Chapter 2 examined modern critical readings of Xenophon as historiographer and philosopher, this final section surveys readings and translations from ancient to modern times, and the differing uses to which Xenophon's work has been put. Different works have spoken to different times, as fashions have changed. This chapter offers some key moments in the history of the reading of Xenophon; the diversity of literary and theoretical responses to his work demonstrates the generic breadth and enduring interest of his work.

Ancient emulation

Xenophon's work was widely circulated and read in antiquity. Plato had clearly read the *Cyropaedia* when he wrote about the decline of Achaemenid monarchy in his *Laws* (3.694a–698a), and when he criticized the model of the shepherd king, but developed the importance of kingly knowledge, in his *Statesman*.[1] Aristotle, too, drew on the *Cyropaedia* as a source of exemplars, with elements of his thought on kingship, on equitable distribution, and friendship in the *Politics* and *Nicomachean Ethics* echoing Xenophon's work, and theorizing his narrative.[2]

For Cicero, Xenophon's work provided important models of effective inspiration for leaders, as the speakers in his dialogues observe. 'Xenophon's books are very useful on many topics; keep reading them, as you do, with care', the elderly Cato advises, before citing Cyrus the Younger's approval of land management as an appropriate task

---

[1] Danzig 2003a; Atack 2018b. See also Chapter 6.
[2] Atack forthcoming.

for leaders.[3] Cicero was aware of Xenophon's work in shaping his exemplars, writing to his brother that Xenophon's account of Cyrus was 'written...not in view of faith to history but as a model of the just exercise of power'.[4] He shows how ancient readers put Xenophon's work to use, embedding a report of how Scipio Africanus, the general responsible for the Romans' defeat of the Carthaginians, and a great hero of the Roman Republic, used Xenophon's work within a larger philosophical discussion of the rather Xenophontic topic of ways of overcoming pain and hardship. Scipio, Cicero writes,

always used to have Xenophon in his hands; among the chief points he made in praising him was that he used to say that the same labours were not equally hard for the general and the ordinary solder, because his status (*honos*) made the task lighter for the general.
(Cic. *Tusc.* 2.62)

Cicero's examples suggest that Xenophon's works, from the *Cyropaedia* to the *Memorabilia*, were well known to the educated elite of the Roman world, including his own circle of correspondents and readers.[5] Xenophon's portraits of Cyrus and Agesilaus fuelled their inclusion in a standard list of founding heroes, kings, and generals.[6]

Xenophon's readers in antiquity also included authors who emulated his work; the writer of exemplars thus became an exemplar himself. Arrian of Nicomedia (*c.*95–175 CE) used Xenophon's writings as a template for a range of works, spanning genres as his predecessor did. These included an account in seven books (like Xenophon's) of Alexander's campaigns in Asia, the *Anabasis of Alexander*, modelled on Xenophon's *Anabasis*, and a hunting manual which echoed and updated the *Cynegeticus*.[7] Where Xenophon began his work on hunting with an account of the origin of hunting with the gods, Arrian started with an explicit acknowledgement of 'Xenophon son of Gryllus'. Arrian felt such a strong connection with his predecessor that he regarded himself as a younger Xenophon, not least because of their

---

[3] Cic. *Sen.* 59; Xen. *Oec.* 4.4–11.

[4] Cicero *Q Fr.* 1.1.23. Elsewhere (*Leg.* 2.56) Cicero is happy to use the *Cyropaedia* as a source of information about Persian burial practices. See Humble 2020: 31–5. I thank Malcolm Schofield for further suggestions on Cicero's use of Xenophon.

[5] References to Cyrus: Cic. *Fam.* 5.12.3, *Q Fr.* 1.1.23, 1.2.7, *Sen.* 30, 32, 79, 81, *Leg.* 2.56, *Rep.* 1.43, *Off.* 2.16; Choice of Hercules: Cic. *Off.* 1.118.

[6] Cic. *Off.* 2.16.

[7] Phillips and Willcock 1999.

mutual love of hunting and philosophy (Arr. *Cyn.* 1.4). In his *Anabasis*, he presents Alexander the Great as a keen reader of Xenophon, who cites the story of the Ten Thousand to encourage his men (Arr. *An.* 2.7.8–9), and uses it as a source of information on Persian tactics (2.8.11).[8] However, Arrian accepts that the analogy between Xenophon's campaign and Alexander's is imperfect: the latter was a leader, not serving in someone else's force as Xenophon did (1.12.4). Arrian asserts his own social position and experience as a qualification for writing about such a great man, and we might wonder whether he mused on Xenophon's qualifications for writing about Cyrus.[9]

Scenes and elements from Xenophon's work were adapted. The first-century CE poet Silius Italicus modified the story of the Choice of Heracles for a key moment in his epic account of the Punic War, not just making the Roman general Scipio a reader of Xenophon but putting him in Heracles' place.[10] Plutarch, writing around the turn of the second century CE, made more direct use of Xenophon's *Constitution of the Spartans* as a source for his lives of Spartan leaders, but he also drew more obliquely on the *Symposium* as a genre for communicating philosophical ideas.[11] Philostratus of Athens, writing a little later, imagined the sophist Apollonius of Tyana invoking the Choice of Heracles when choosing between philosophical schools.[12]

The late antique biographer Eunapius of Sardis, educated in Athens and writing in the fourth century CE, opens his *Lives of the Philosophers and Sophists* with a discussion of Xenophon's writing and its influence, continuing the trend of later authors regarding Xenophon as a model for themselves and comparing his subjects with their subjects. Eunapius takes it for granted that Alexander learned useful lessons from Xenophon, but also considers Xenophon to be a unique model in that his words were matched by his actions.[13] The idealized withdrawal of philosophers from politics to quiet lives of contemplation made Xenophon's life of action impossible for philosophers of Eunapius' time to emulate; and his reportage of both small and great deeds also made him difficult for writers themselves to emulate.

---

[8] On Arrian's interactions with Xenophon's *Anabasis*, see Miltsios 2022; Strazdins 2022.
[9] Gray 1990.
[10] Sil. *Pun.* 15.68–120; Bull 2006: 97.
[11] C. Cooper; Gengler 2020.
[12] Philostr. *V A* 6.11.3–8. I thank Phil Horky for this point.
[13] Eunap. *VS* 453.

Exemplarity and esotericism

As Arrian's use of Xenophon might suggest, writers from antiquity onwards provided advice for the powerful by elaborating case studies from the classical past. Xenophon's accounts of leadership stand at the head of a long tradition of instructional works, in a genre often referred to as *speculum principis* ('mirror for the prince'), spanning the period from classical antiquity to early modernity, and the European and Asian worlds.[14] Cyrus was an exemplar idealized across cultures. The Renaissance saw a renewed enthusiasm for including exemplars from classical antiquity in these works, alongside strongly voiced concern that figures from the pagan past were not suitable models for Christian princes.[15] Instruction manuals for the rulers of city states proliferated, filled with examples from the classical literature which was being disseminated more widely both in Greek and, more accessibly, in Latin and vernacular translations.[16]

Scholars inside and outside the Christian churches produced custom editions of translations of Xenophon's work as gifts for the powerful, for both popes and kings. The humanist Francesco Filelfo (1398–1481) dedicated his translation of the *Cyropaedia* to Pope Paul II; in addition to a sumptuous manuscript version, a print edition was published in 1477.[17] Cardinal Bessarion translated the *Memorabilia*, again circulated as a manuscript and a little later as a printed book.[18] A complete Greek text of Xenophon's works was published by the Aldine Press in Venice in 1525, but translations reached a broader elite readership.[19]

The most influential reader of Xenophon, Niccolò Machiavelli (1469–1527), the political theorist and administrator in turbulent Florence, was a critical participant in this tradition, using Xenophon's exemplars in his own version of the mirror for princes, *The Prince*.[20] He noted the way in which great leaders used the examples of their predecessors, remarking that Scipio's ethics and actions drew on his

---

[14] See Tatum 1989: 4–9. On the genre across cultures, see Blaydes et al. 2018; in relation to Cyrus, see Grogan 2014: 37–69.

[15] Grogan 2007: 65.

[16] Humble 2017.

[17] Filelfo 1477.

[18] Bodleian MS. Canon. Class. Lat. 131.

[19] Asulanus 1525. The *Hellenica* had been included in an earlier volume of historical texts: Gemistus 1503.

[20] Machiavelli 1970, 1988.

imitation of the model provided by Xenophon's Cyrus. The latter becomes one of Machiavelli's core examples; he represents the kind of ruler who expands his domain through conquest. He also appears along with Caesar and Alexander as a ruler who could be generous with goods acquired through conquest, and along with Moses and Theseus as a liberator of his people.[21] Machiavelli's use of Xenophon has been particularly influential on later interpreters, because it has led political theorists to read Xenophon through a Machiavellian lens and to see the latter's often brutal *realpolitik* lurking beneath Xenophon's descriptions of virtuous rulers.[22]

However, Machiavelli's use of Xenophon is not representative of the early modern response to his work; more conventional accounts of courtly virtue also drew on Xenophon's philosophy of good leadership. Beyond Italy, Xenophon's work circulated in the Tudor and Stuart courts in various translations; it was translated into English by William Barker, a tutor to the powerful Howard family, who dedicated two versions, in 1552 and 1567, to powerful men whose patronage he sought.[23] Admirers sought out depictions of the Choice of Hercules.[24]

The novelist Sarah Fielding's English translation of the *Memorabilia* and *Apology, Memoirs of Socrates*, was first published in 1762 and went into multiple editions.[25] Fielding wrote in her preface:

That the Memoirs of Socrates, with regard to the greatest part, are held in the highest estimation, is most certain; and if there are some passages which seem obscure; and of which the use doth not so plainly appear to us at this distance of time, and from the dissimilarity of our customs and manners; yet, perhaps, we might not do amiss, in taking Socrates himself for our example in this particular, as well as in many others...

Her translation, described by Edith Hall as 'graceful, lucid, and accurate', achieved continuing commercial success, and her rendering of the *Apology* was republished by the Everyman library, aimed at a wide general readership, over a century later.[26]

Among the founding fathers of the USA, Xenophon's Socratic works were seen as the best source for Socrates and the educational tradition

---

[21] Machiavelli 1988: chs 6, 16, 26.
[22] Rasmussen 2009.
[23] Grogan 2007, 2020.
[24] Rood 2017a.
[25] Fielding 1762.
[26] Hall 2016: 128.

he represented.[27] Thomas Ricks, exploring the founding fathers' reading of Xenophon, notes the importance of farming to both readers and
author.[28] But another overlap between the early USA and classical
Athens was the problematic question of chattel slavery. One might
question whether the moral lessons the young nation's leaders took
from Xenophon incorporated the ready acceptance of slavery and the
equation of enslaved status with lack of virtue featured in the Socratic
works.

As a young man, Benjamin Franklin (1706–90) bought and read
'Xenophon's *Memorable Things of Socrates*', in Edward Bysshe's 1712
English translation.[29] He was following up a mention of the Socratic
method in an English grammar book. Having read the text, he was
moved to change his whole approach to speaking; he wrote: 'I was
charmed with it, adopted it, dropt my abrupt contradiction and positive
argumentation, and put on the humble inquirer and doubter'.[30] Early
in his career, Franklin translated the discussions on leadership between
Socrates, Glaucon, and Charmides (*Mem.* 3.6–7) as 'Public Men', and
published his own dialogue 'Concerning Virtue and Pleasure' in
imitation.[31] Thomas Jefferson (1743–1826) also found inspiration in
the *Memorabilia*, as a means of accessing the thought of Socrates:
'Of Socrates we have nothing genuine but in the *Memorabilia* of
Xenophon,' he wrote, criticizing Plato for attributing his own
'whimsies' to his teacher.[32]

But not everyone took Xenophon quite so seriously. Laurence Sterne
invoked the *Cyropaedia* as an example misused by the father of the
protagonist of his rambling novel *Tristram Shandy* (1759–67), who
begins, and fails to complete, a '*Tristrapaedia*' about his son's upbring-
ing.[33] While Sterne's novel is shot through with classical learning, it
offers a counter-example to Xenophon's exemplary account of personal
development.

[27] Humble 2017.
[28] Ricks 2020: 81–2.
[29] Bysshe 1712, with many subsequent editions; the volume drew on François Charpentier's
1650 French translation and included the latter's short biographical sketch.
[30] Franklin 1887: 50.
[31] Franklin 1887: 383–404.
[32] Thomas Jefferson, 'Letter to William Short, 31 October 1819', cited in Ricks 2020: 82.
[33] Sterne 1967, e.g. vol. 5, chs 16, 26; Tatum 1989: 3–4, Humble 2017: 431–2.

Xenophon, classics, and colonialism

In the nineteenth century and the era of colonial expansion, the *Anabasis* spoke to British imperialism and to American westward expansion.[34] Both location and situation resonated with those being educated to administer and control annexed and occupied territories, both in the American west and in the world east and south of Europe. Classical languages and literature remained an important part of elite education, and Xenophon's Greek was treated as particularly useful for learners, while his subject matter remained relevant. The *Anabasis* became the text which combined linguistic pedagogy and imperial aims, replacing the *Cyropaedia* and the *Memorabilia* as the author's key work. School editions proliferated, and it was excerpted and adapted for teaching purposes.[35]

As the precise region of Xenophon's travels became the focus of a global geopolitical crisis, contemporary writers picked up the idea of the 'march upcountry' as a framework for narratives of invasion – and of retreat. Writers of speculative fiction have taken Xenophon's ideas beyond the geography of this planet to encompass military narratives set in imagined communities across space.

Philosophical critics of Xenophon often focused on what they saw as his lack of philosophical acuity and originality, compared with Plato's works, which were taken to contain the more accurate depiction of Socrates' thought. Friedrich Schleiermacher, writing in the early nineteenth century, was one of the first to express this view, which became an unexamined commonplace among scholars of ancient philosophy.[36] John Burnet cast doubt on Xenophon's knowledge of Socrates' thought, and pointed to his dependence on Plato's work.[37] Despite damning Xenophon in his earlier work, Gregory Vlastos later pointed to the *Symposium* and the account of Theodote (*Mem.* 3.11) as evidence of the sophistication of Xenophon's Socrates.[38]

The political philosopher Leo Strauss played a large part in Xenophon's mid-twentieth-century rehabilitation. Strauss had a specific agenda, seeking 'timeless' wisdom from ancient writers in

---

[34] Rood 2010.
[35] Rijksbaron 2002; Rood 2004b: 43–50.
[36] Schleiermacher 1987, originally published 1815, with English translation in Hare 1832–3: ii.538–55.
[37] Burnet 1911: xiii–xxiii.
[38] Vlastos 1957: 498–500, 1991: 30; see Morrison 1987.

preference to what he saw as a decadent modernity.[39] However, he regarded this wisdom as obscured from general view; because philosophers like Socrates were persecuted by the state, they hid their wisdom, so that it was only communicated to readers with the training and knowledge to uncover the true account beneath the text's surface. This reading developed a version of Xenophon who could easily be seen as a predecessor of political theorists such as Niccolò Machiavelli.[40]

Virtue and leadership reunited

As the earlier chapters have shown, the revival in scholarly interest in Xenophon has led to a flowering of insight and interpretation. One aspect of reading Xenophon which has enjoyed a recent surge is his interest in leadership, and the personal qualities which made Cyrus and others successful and popular as generals and rulers. While political theorists have often framed Xenophon as a realist in the manner of Machiavelli, social scientists and philosophers have connected his thought with another resurgent strand of theory drawing on classical antiquity: virtue ethics. Xenophon's work has even been incorporated into management studies, a discipline in which exemplarity continues to be an important method. Episodes from his work, from Clearchus' generalship to the Choice of Heracles, feature in a series of case studies in 'Ancient Leadership'.[41] Xenophon's Cyrus has been invoked here for his Socratic, ethical approach to leadership.[42]

These strands intersected in the later work of the theorist Michel Foucault, whose 'genealogical' method involved exploring the long history of concepts and identifying moments of structural change, as well as a concern with ordering and organization.[43] His *History of Sexuality* sought to understand how an individual's sexuality became their defining characteristic; during the course of researching it, Foucault turned to classical antiquity as the location of a distinctive

---

[39] L. Strauss 1959; see also Dorion 2001.
[40] Rasmussen 2009.
[41] For example Tamiolaki 2019, 2020a.
[42] Sandridge 2012.
[43] Foucault 1977.

culture.[44] He found Xenophon's *Oeconomicus* important for its depiction of ancient married life, in which 'the husband's self-restraint pertains to an art of governing – governing in general, governing oneself and governing a wife who must be kept under control and respected at the same time'.[45] But Foucault's use of Xenophon's framework extended more broadly across his later work, in which the idea of the 'care of the self' (*souci de soi*) draws heavily on Xenophontic ideas of self-control and *epimeleia*.[46] Foucauldian ideas of governmentality as applied to the self can be seen as a development of Xenophon's orderly structures.[47]

These recent readings show that, despite his apparent conservatism and adherence to convention, Xenophon's thought can inspire a wide range of responses. Contemporary readers have used his writings productively to gain a better understanding of the societies within which he lived, and to generate reflections on their own lives and times in different political circumstances around the globe, where democracy and tyranny remain in tension.

---

[44] Foucault 1984–6. See Jarratt 2014; Elden 2016: 134–63.
[45] Foucault 1984–6: ii.165. See Foxhall 1994.
[46] Foucault 1984–6: iii.50.
[47] Foucault 1984–6: vol. 2; Elden 2016.

BIBLIOGRAPHY

Anderson, J. K. 1974. *Xenophon*. London, Duckworth.

Andrewes, A. 1974. 'The Arginousai Trial', *Phoenix* 28: 112–22.

Asulanus, F. 1525. *Xenophōntos hapanta ta heuriskomena = Xenophontis omnia, qvae extant*. Venice: Aldus.

Atack, C. 2018a. '"Cyrus appeared both great and good": Xenophon and the Performativity of Kingship', in P. Christesen, D. S. Allen, and P. Millett (eds.), *How to Do Things with History. New Approaches to Ancient Greece*. Oxford, Oxford University Press: 109–35.

——. 2018b. 'Plato's Statesman and Xenophon's Cyrus', in Danzig et al. 2018: 510–43.

——. 2018c. 'Politeia and the Past in Xenophon and Isocrates', *Trends in Classics* 10: 171–94.

——. 2020a. *The Discourse of Kingship in Classical Greece*. London, Routledge.

——. 2020b. 'Plato's Queer Time: Dialogic Moments in the Life and Death of Socrates', *Classical Receptions Journal* 12: 10–31.

——. 2020c. 'The Shepherd King and His Flock: Paradoxes of Leadership and Care in Classical Greek Philosophy', in L. Tomkins (ed.), *Paradox and Power in Caring Leadership. Critical and Philosophical Reflections*. Cheltenham, Edward Elgar: 75–85.

——. 2021. 'Citizenship and Gender', in C. Atack and P. Cartledge (eds.), *A Cultural History of Democracy in Antiquity*. London, Bloomsbury Academic: 115–35.

——. 2022. 'Xenophon's Moral Luck: Crisis and Leadership Opportunity in *Anabasis* 3', in Rood and Tamiolaki 2022: 63–83.

——. 2023a. 'Ambiguities of Despotic Power in Xenophon's *Cyropaedia*', *Cahiers 'Mondes anciens'* 17: n.p.

——. 2023b. 'Exemplarity and the Practice of Charisma in Athenian Stories of Leadership', in J.-P. Guilhembet, R. Laignoux, and P. Montlahuc (eds.), *Le Charisme en politique. Max Weber face à l'Antiquité grecque et romaine*. Rome, Publications de l'École française de Rome: 121–53.

——. 2024. '"By Zeus," Said Theodote: Women as Interlocutors and Performers in Xenophon's Philosophical Writing', in S. Brill and C. McKeen (eds.), *The Routledge Handbook of Women and Ancient Greek Philosophy*. New York, Routledge: 118–34.

——. forthcoming. 'Aristotle's Reception of Xenophon', in D. Gish and C. A. Farrell (eds.), *Brill's Companion to the Reception of Xenophon*. Leiden: Brill.

Azoulay, V. 2004. 'The Medo-Persian Ceremonial: Xenophon, Cyrus and the King's Body', in Tuplin and Azoulay 2004: 147–73.

———. 2007. 'Panthée, Mania et quelques autres: les jeux du genre dans l'oeuvre de Xénophon', in V. Sebillotte Cuchet and N. Ernoult (eds.), *Problèmes du genre en Grèce ancienne*. Paris: Publications de la Sorbonne: 277–87.

———. 2018a. *Xenophon and the Graces of Power. A Greek Guide to Political Manipulation*. Edited and translated by A. Krieger. Swansea, Classical Press of Wales. First published in French 2004.

———. 2018b. 'Xénophon et la redéfinition de la philia', in M. Crubellier, A. Jaulin, and P. Pellegrin (eds.), *Philia et dikè. Aspects du lien social et politique en Grèce ancienne*. Paris, Classiques Garnier: 101–21.

———. 2020. 'Sparta and the *Cyropaedia*: The Correct Use of Analogies', in A. Powell and N. Richer (eds.), *Xenophon and Sparta*. Swansea, Classical Press of Wales: 129–59.

———. and Ismard, P. 2020. *Athènes 403. Une histoire chorale*. Paris: Flammarion.

Badian, E. 2004. 'Xenophon the Athenian', in Tuplin and Azoulay 2004: 33–53.

Baragwanath, E. 2002. 'Xenophon's Foreign Wives', *Prudentia* 34: 125–58.

———. 2012. 'The Wonder of Freedom: Xenophon on Slavery', in F. Hobden and C. Tuplin (eds.), *Xenophon. Ethical Principles and Historical Inquiry*. Leiden, Brill: 631–63.

———. 2016. 'Panthea's Sisters: Negotiating East–West Polarities through Gender in Xenophon', *CW* 109: 165–78.

———. 2017. 'The Character and Function of Speeches in Xenophon', in Flower 2017: 279–97.

———. 2022. 'A Universalist Moral Compass: Depicting Greeks and Foreigners in Anabasis 5 and 6', in Rood and Tamiolaki 2022: 131–55.

———. forthcoming. *Xenophon's Women*.

Baragwanath, E. and Verity, A. 2022. *Xenophon. Estate Management and Symposium*. Oxford, Oxford University Press.

Benson, H. H. 2010. 'Socratic Method', in D. Morrison (ed.), *The Cambridge Companion to Socrates*. Cambridge, Cambridge University Press: 179–200.

Berkel, T. A. van. 2020. *The Economics of Friendship. Conceptions of Reciprocity in Classical Greece*. Leiden, Brill.

Berlin, I. 1969. *Four Essays on Liberty*. Oxford, Oxford University Press.

Bigwood, J. M. 1983. 'The Ancient Accounts of the Battle of Cunaxa', *AJPh* 104: 340–57.

Blaydes, L., Grimmer, J., and McQueen, A. 2018. 'Mirrors for Princes and Sultans: Advice on the Art of Governance in the Medieval Christian and Islamic Worlds', *Journal of Politics* 80: 1150–67.

Bloch, D. 2004. 'The Date of Xenophon's *Poroï*', *C&M* 55: 5–16.

Blundell, M. W. 1991. *Helping Friends and Harming Enemies. A Study in Sophocles and Greek Ethics.* Cambridge, Cambridge University Press.

Bonazzi, M. 2020. *The Sophists.* Cambridge, Cambridge University Press.

Bordes, J. 1982. *Politeia dans la pensée grecque jusqu'à Aristote.* Paris, Les Belles Lettres.

Bourriot, F. 1995. *Kalos kagathos, kalokagathia. D'un terme de propagande de sophistes à une notion sociale et philosophique. Étude d'histoire athénienne.* 2 vols. Hildesheim, G. Olms.

Bowden, H. 2013. 'On Kissing and Making Up: Court Protocol and Historiography in Alexander the Great's "Experiment with Proskynesis"', *BICS* 56: 55–77.

Brennan, S. 2022. *Xenophon's Anabasis. A Socratic History.* Edinburgh, Edinburgh University Press.

Brennan, S. and Thomas, D. (eds.) 2021. *The Landmark Xenophon's Anabasis.* New York: Pantheon.

Briant, P. 2002. *From Cyrus to Alexander. A History of the Persian Empire.* Translated by P. T. Daniels. Winona Lake, IN, Eisenbrauns. First published in French 1996.

Brock, R. 2004. 'Xenophon's Political Imagery', in Tuplin and Azoulay 2004: 247–57.

———. 2013. *Greek Political Imagery from Homer to Aristotle.* London, Bloomsbury.

Brownson, C. L. 1922. *Xenophon. Anabasis, Books IV–VII.* Loeb Classical Library. Cambridge, MA, Harvard University Press.

Bull, M. 2006. [2005], *The Mirror of the Gods: classical mythology in Renaissance art.* London, Penguin.

Burnet, J. 1911. *Plato's Phaedo.* Oxford, Clarendon Press.

Burns, T. (ed.) 2015. *Brill's Companion to Leo Strauss' Writings on Classical Political Thought.* Leiden, Brill.

Buzzetti, E. 2014. *Xenophon the Socratic Prince. The Argument of the Anabasis of Cyrus.* Basingstoke, Palgrave Macmillan.

Bysshe, E. 1712. *The Memorable Things of Socrates, Written by Xenophon...Translated into English. To which are Prefix'd the Life of Socrates, from the French of Monsieur Charpentier...and the Life of Xenophon.* London, G. Sawbridge.

Cammack, D. 2021. 'Deliberation and Discussion in Classical Athens', *Journal of Political Philosophy* 29: 135–66.

Carter, L. B. 1986. *The Quiet Athenian.* Oxford, Clarendon Press.

Cartledge, P. 1981. 'Spartan Wives: Liberation or Licence?', *CQ* 31: 84–105.

———. 1987. *Agesilaos and the Crisis of Sparta*. London, Duckworth.

———. 2002. *Sparta and Lakonia. A Regional History, 1300–362* BC. Second edition. London, Routledge.

———. 2016. *Democracy. A Life*. Oxford, Oxford University Press.

———. (ed.) and Waterfield, R. (trans.) 1997. *Xenophon. Hiero the Tyrant and Other Treatises*. London, Penguin.

Cawkwell, G. L. 1963. 'Eubulus', *JHS* 83: 47–67.

———. 1973. 'The Foundation of the Second Athenian Confederacy', *CQ* 23: 47–60.

———. (ed.) and Warner, R. (trans.) 1979. *Xenophon. A History of My Times (Hellenica)*. Harmondsworth, Penguin.

Christ, M. R. 2006. *The Bad Citizen in Classical Athens*. Cambridge, Cambridge University Press.

———. 2020. *Xenophon and the Athenian Democracy. The Education of an Elite Citizenry*. Cambridge, Cambridge University Press.

Collins, J. H. 2015. *Exhortations to Philosophy. The Protreptics of Plato, Isocrates, and Aristotle*. New York, Oxford University Press.

Connor, W. R. 1977. 'Tyrannis polis', in J. H. D'Arms and J. W. Eadie (eds.), *Ancient and Modern. Essays in Honor of Gerald F. Else*. Ann Arbor, MI, Center for Coordination of Ancient & Modern Studies, University of Michigan: 95–109.

Cooper, C. 2020. 'Sympotic Intertextuality in Plutarch's *Maxime cum principibus philosopho esse disserendum*', in T. S. Schmidt, M. Vamvouri, and R. Hirsch-Luipold (eds.), *The Dynamics of Intertextuality in Plutarch*. Leiden, Brill: 307–23.

Cooper, J. M. 1977. 'Aristotle on the Forms of Friendship', *Review of Metaphysics* 30: 619–48.

Cox, C. A. 2010. 'Marriage in Ancient Athens', in B. Rawson (ed.), *A Companion to Families in the Greek and Roman Worlds*. Chichester, Blackwell: 231–44.

Danzig, G. 2003a. 'Did Plato read Xenophon's *Cyropaedia?*', in S. Scolnicov and L. Brisson (eds.), *Plato's Laws. From Theory into Practice. Proceedings of the VI Symposium Platonicum*. Sankt Augustin, Academia: 286–97.

———. 2003b. 'Why Socrates Was Not a Farmer: Xenophon's *Oeconomicus* as a Philosophical Dialogue', *G&R* 50: 57–76.

———. 2005. 'Intra-Socratic Polemics: The Symposia of Plato and Xenophon', *GRBS* 45: 331–57.

———. 2009. 'Big Boys and Little Boys: Justice and Law in Xenophon's *Cyropaedia* and *Memorabilia*', *Polis* 26: 271–95.

————. 2014. 'Alcibiades versus Pericles: Apologetic Strategies in Xenophon's *Memorabilia*', *G&R* 61: 7–28.

————. 2017. 'Xenophon and the Socratic Elenchos: The Verbal Thrashing as a Tool for Instilling Sophrosune', *AncPhil* 37: 293–318.

————., Johnson, D. M., and Morrison, D. (eds.) 2018. *Plato and Xenophon. Comparative Studies*. Mnemosyne Supplements. Leiden, Brill.

Davies, J. K. 1971. *Athenian Propertied Families, 600–300 B.C.* Oxford, Clarendon Press.

Degen, J. 2019. 'Xenophon and the Light from Heaven', *AHB* 33: 81–107.

————. 2020. 'Ancient Near Eastern Traditions in Xenophon's *Cyropaedia*: Conceptions of Royal Qualities and Empire', in B. Jacobs (ed.), *Ancient Information on Persia Re-assessed. Xenophon's Cyropaedia. Proceedings of a Conference Held at Marburg in Honour of Christopher J. Tuplin, December 1–2, 2017*. Classica et Orientalia. Wiesbaden, Harrassowitz: 197–240.

Delebecque, E. 1957. *Essai sur la vie de Xénophon*. Paris, Klincksieck.

Detienne, M. and Vernant, J.-P. 1974. *Les Ruses de l'intelligence. La métis des grecs*. Paris, Flammarion.

Dewald, C. 2003. 'Form and Content: The Question of Tyranny in Herodotus', in Morgan 2003: 25–58.

Dillery, J. 1995. *Xenophon and the History of His Times*. London, Routledge.

Dorion, L.-A. 2001. 'L'exégèse straussienne de Xénophon: le cas paradigmatique de *Mémorables* IV 4', *PhilosAnt* 1: 87–118.

————. 2004. 'Socrate et la *basilikê tekhnê*: essai d'exégèse comparative', in V. Karasmanis (ed.), *Socrates. 2400 Years Since His Death (399 B.C.– 2001 A.D.)*. Athens: European Cultural Centre of Delphi: 51–62.

————. 2008. 'Héraklès entre Prodicos et Xénophon', *PhilosAnt* 8: 85–114.

————. 2010. 'The Straussian Exegesis of Xenophon: The Paradigmatic Case of *Memorabilia* IV 4', in V. J. Gray (ed.), *Xenophon*. Oxford, Oxford University Press: 283–323.

————. 2013. *L'Autre Socrate. Études sur les écrits socratiques de Xénophon*. Paris, Les Belles Lettres.

————. 2017. 'Xenophon and Greek Philosophy', in Flower 2017: 37–56.

————. and Bandini, M. 2000–11. *Xénophon. Mémorables*. 3 vols. Paris, Les Belles Lettres.

————. 2021. *Xénophon. Hiéron*. Paris, Les Belles Lettres.

Dover, K. J. 2016. *Greek Homosexuality*. New edition. London, Bloomsbury. First published 1978.

Ducat, J. 2006. *Spartan Education. Youth and Society in the Classical Period*. Swansea, Classical Press of Wales.

Due, B. 1983. 'The Trial of the Generals in Xenophon's *Hellenica*', *C&M* 34: 33–44.

———. 1989. *The Cyropaedia. Xenophon's Aims and Methods*. Aarhus, Aarhus University Press.

Durnerin, M. 2022. 'Information et pouvoir au prisme de Xénophon'. PhD thesis, École Normale Supérieure de Lyon.

Elden, S. 2016. *Foucault's Last Decade*. Cambridge, Polity Press.

Ellis, A. 2016. 'A Socratic History: Theology in Xenophon's Rewriting of Herodotus' Croesus *Logos*', *JHS* 136: 73–91.

Erbse, H. 1961. 'Die Architektonik im Aufbau von Xenophons *Memorabilien*', *Hermes* 89: 257–87.

Farrell, C. A. 2016. 'Xenophon *Poroi* 5', *Polis* 33: 331–55.

Fielding, S. 1762. *Xenophon's Memoirs of Socrates with The Defence of Socrates, before His Judges*. Bath: C. Pope.

Filelfo, F. 1477. *Praefatio in Xenophontis libros de Cyri paedia ad Paulum secundum Pontificem Maximum*. Milan: Simon Magniagus.

Finley, M. I. 1962. 'Athenian Demagogues', *P&P* 21: 3–24.

Fisher, N. R. E. 1992. *Hybris. A Study in the Values of Honour and Shame in Ancient Greece*. Warminster, Aris & Phillips.

Flower, M. A. 2012. *Xenophon's Anabasis, or The Expedition of Cyrus*. Oxford, Oxford University Press.

———. 2015. 'Implied Characterization and the Meaning of History in Xenophon's *Hellenica*', in R. Ash, J. Mossman, and F. B. Titchener (eds.), *Fame and Infamy. Essays on Characterization in Greek and Roman Biography and Historiography*. Oxford, Oxford University Press: 110–27.

———. (ed.) 2017. *The Cambridge Companion to Xenophon*. Cambridge, Cambridge University Press.

Foucault, M. 1977. 'Nietzsche, Genealogy, History', in D. F. Bouchard (ed.), *Language, Counter-Memory, Practice. Selected Essays and Interviews*. Translated by D. F. Bouchard and S. Simon. Ithaca, NY, Cornell University Press: 139–64.

———. 1984–6. *The History of Sexuality*. Translated by R. Hurley, 3 vols. Harmondsworth, Penguin. First published in French 1976–84.

Foxhall, L. 1994. 'Pandora Unbound: A Feminist Critique of Foucault's History of Sexuality', in A. Cornwall and N. Lindisfarne (eds.), *Dislocating Masculinity. Comparative Ethnographies*. London, Routledge: 133–46.

Franklin, B. 1887. *The Works of Benjamin Franklin, Vol. I. Autobiography, Letters and Misc. Writings 1725–1734*. Edited by J. Bigelow. New York, G. P. Putnam's Sons.

Fuks, A. 1971. *The Ancestral Constitution. Four Studies in Athenian Party Politics at the End of the Fifth Century B.C.* Westport, CT, Greenwood Press.

Gauthier, P. 1976. *Un Commentaire historique des Poroi de Xénophon.* Paris, Droz.

Gehrke, H.-J. 2023. *The Greeks and Their Histories. Myth, History, and Society.* Translated by R. Geuss. Cambridge, Cambridge University Press, 2023. First published in German 2014.

Gemistus, G. 1503. *Xenophōntos paraleipomena, haper kai Hellēnika ekalese...* Venice, Aldus Manutius.

Gengler, O. 2020. 'Plutarch's and Xenophon's Sparta: Intra- and Intertextual Relations in the Spartan Lives', in T. S. Schmidt, M. Vamvouri, and R. Hirsch-Luipold (eds.), *The Dynamics of Intertextuality in Plutarch.* Leiden, Brill: 111–28.

Gera, D. L. 1993. *Xenophon's Cyropaedia. Style, Genre, and Literary Technique.* Oxford, Clarendon Press.

Gilhuly, K. 2024. 'The History of Sexuality in Xenophon's *Symposium*', in K. Gilhuly and J. P. Ulrich (eds.), *Making Time for Greek and Roman Literature.* New York, Routledge: 62–83.

Gish, D. A. 2009. 'Spartan Justice: The Conspiracy of Kinadon in Xenophon's *Hellenika*', *Polis* 26: 339–69.

Glazebrook, A. 2009. 'Cosmetics and *Sôphrosunê*: Ischomachos' Wife in Xenophon's *Oikonomikos*', *CW* 102: 233–48.

———. and Olson, K. 2013. 'Greek and Roman Marriage', in T. K. Hubbard (ed.), *A Companion to Greek and Roman Sexualities.* Hoboken, NJ, John Wiley & Sons: 69–82.

Goldhill, S. D. 1998. 'The Seductions of the Gaze: Socrates and His Girlfriends', in P. Cartledge, P. Millett, and S. von Reden (eds.), *Kosmos. Essays in Order, Conflict and Community in Classical Athens.* Cambridge, Cambridge University Press: 105–24.

Gray, V. J. 1986. 'Xenophon's *Hiero* and the Meeting of the Wise Man and Tyrant in Greek Literature', *CQ*, 36: 115–23.

———. 1989. *The Character of Xenophon's Hellenica.* London, Duckworth.

———. 1990. 'The Moral Interpretation of the "Second Preface" to Arrian's *Anabasis*', *JHS* 110: 180–6.

———. 1998. *The Framing of Socrates. The Literary Interpretation of Xenophon's Memorabilia.* Stuttgart, F. Steiner.

———. 2006. 'The Linguistic Philosophies of Prodicus in Xenophon's "Choice of Heracles"', *CQ* 56: 426–35.

———. (ed.) 2007. *Xenophon on Government.* Cambridge, Cambridge University Press.

———. 2011a. 'Thucydides' Source Citations: "It is said"', *CQ* 61: 75–90.

———. 2011b. *Xenophon's Mirror of Princes. Reading the Reflections.* Oxford, Oxford University Press.

———. 2011c. 'Xenophon's Socrates and Democracy', *Polis* 28: 1–32.

———. 2016. 'Herodotus (and Ctesias) Re-enacted: Leadership in Xenophon's *Cyropaedia*', in J. Priestley and V. Zali (eds.), *Brill's Companion to the Reception of Herodotus in Antiquity and Beyond.* Leiden, Brill: 301–21.

———. 2017. 'Xenophon's Language and Expression', in Flower 2017: 223–40.

Griffith, M. (ed.) 2000. *Sophocles. Antigone.* Cambridge, Cambridge University Press.

Grogan, J. 2007. '"Many Cyruses": Xenophon's *Cyropaedia* and English Renaissance Humanism', *Hermathena* 183: 63–74.

———. 2014. *The Persian Empire in English Renaissance Writing, 1549–1622.* Basingstoke, Palgrave Macmillan.

———. (ed.) 2020. *William Barker. Xenophon's Cyropaedia.* Cambridge, Modern Humanities Research Association.

Hall, E. 2016. 'Intellectual Pleasure and the Woman Translator in Seventeenth- and Eighteenth-Century England', in E. Hall and R. Wyles (eds.), *Women Classical Scholars. Unsealing the Fountain from the Renaissance to Jacqueline de Romilly.* Oxford, Oxford University Press: 103–31.

Hammond, M. (trans.) and Atack, C. (ed.) 2023. *Memories of Socrates. Xenophon's Memorabilia and Apology.* Oxford, Oxford University Press.

Hansen, M. H. 1999. *The Athenian Democracy in the Age of Demosthenes. Structure, Principles, and Ideology.* Second edition. Bristol, Bristol Classical Press. First published 1984.

Hare, J. C. (ed.) 1832–3. *The Philological Museum.* 2 vols. Cambridge, J. Smith for Deightons.

Harman, R. 2008. 'Viewing, Power and Interpretation in Xenophon's *Cyropaedia*', in J. Pigon (ed.), *The Children of Herodotus.* Newcastle, Cambridge Scholars Publishing: 69–91.

———. 2023. *The Politics of Viewing in Xenophon's Historical Narratives.* London, Bloomsbury Academic.

Harrison, T. 2003. 'Upside Down and Back to Front: Herodotus and the Greek Encounter with Egypt', in R. Matthews and C. Römer (eds.), *Ancient Perspectives on Egypt.* London, UCL Press: 145–55.

Harvey, F. D. 1965. 'Two Kinds of Equality', *C&M* 26: 101–46.

Hau, L. I. 2016. *Moral History from Herodotus to Diodorus Siculus.* Edinburgh, Edinburgh University Press.

Haubold, J. 2015. '"Shepherds of the People": Greek and Mesopotamian Perspectives', in R. Rollinger and E. van Dongen (eds.),

Mesopotamia in the Ancient World. Impact, Continuities, Parallels. Münster, Ugarit: 245–54.

Henderson, J. 2012. 'Pheraulas Is the Answer, What Was the Question? (You Cannot Be Cyrus)', in F. Hobden and C. Tuplin (eds.), *Xenophon. Ethical Principles and Historical Enquiry.* Leiden, Brill: 541–62.

Henry, M. M. 1995. *Prisoner of History. Aspasia of Miletus and Her Biographical Tradition.* Oxford, Oxford University Press.

Hesk, J. 2000. *Deception and Democracy in Classical Athens.* Cambridge, Cambridge University Press.

Higgins, W. E. 1977. *Xenophon the Athenian. The Problem of the Individual and the Society of the Polis.* Albany, NY, State University of New York Press.

Hirsch, S. W. 1985. *The Friendship of the Barbarians. Xenophon and the Persian Empire.* Hanover, NH, University Press of New England.

Hobden, F. 2005. 'Reading Xenophon's *Symposium*', *Ramus* 34: 93–111.

———. 2017. 'Xenophon's *Oeconomicus*', in Flower 2017: 152–73.

Hoekstra, K. 2016. 'Athenian Democracy and Popular Tyranny', in R. Bourke and Q. Skinner (eds.), *Popular Sovereignty in Historical Perspective.* Cambridge, Cambridge University Press: 15–51.

Horky, P. S. 2021. 'Law and Justice among the Socratics: Contexts for Plato's *Republic*', *Polis* 38: 399–419.

Horn, C. 2012. 'Why Two Epochs of Human History? On the Myth of the *Statesman*', in C. Collobert, P. Destrée, and F. J. Gonzalez (eds.), *Plato And Myth. Studies on the Use and Status of Platonic Myths.* Mnemosyne Supplements. Leiden, Brill: 393–417.

Hornblower, S. 2000. 'Sticks, Stones, and Spartans: The Sociology of Spartan Violence', in H. van Wees (ed.), *War and Violence in Ancient Greece.* Swansea, Classical Press of Wales: 57–82.

———. 2004. '"This was decided" (*edoxe tauta*): The Army as Polis in Xenophon's *Anabasis* – and Elsewhere', in Lane Fox 2004: 243–63.

Huitink, L. and Rood, T. 2016. 'Subordinate Officers in Xenophon's *Anabasis*', *Histos Supplement*, 199–242.

———. (eds.) 2019. *Xenophon. Anabasis. Book III.* Cambridge, Cambridge University Press.

Humble, N. 2004. 'The Author, Date and Purpose of Chapter 14 of the *Lakedaimoniôn Politeia*', in Tuplin and Azoulay 2004: 215–28.

———. 2017. 'Xenophon and the Instruction of Princes', in Flower 2017: 416–34.

———. 2020. 'The Well-Thumbed Attic Muse: Cicero and the Reception of Xenophon's Persia in the Early Modern Period', in J. Grogan (ed.), *Beyond Greece and Rome. Reading the Ancient Near East in Early Modern Europe.* Oxford, Oxford University Press, 29–52.

————. 2022. *Xenophon of Athens. A Socratic on Sparta*. Cambridge, Cambridge University Press.

Huss, B. 1999a. 'The Dancing Sokrates and the Laughing Xenophon, or the Other "Symposium"', *AJPhil* 120: 381–409.

————. 1999b. *Xenophons Symposion. Ein Kommentar*. Stuttgart, Teubner.

Illarraga, R. 2021. 'What the Rulers Want: Xenophon on Cyrus' Psychology', *CQ* 71: 170–82.

————. 2023. 'Notes on the Dynamics between Kingship and Tyranny in Xenophon', in C. Mársico and D. R. Nunes Lopes (eds.), *Xenophon, the Philosopher. Argumentation and Ethics*. Berlin, Peter Lang: 97–110.

Irwin, T. 1974. 'Review of *Xenophon's Socrates*, by Leo Strauss', *Philosophical Review* 83: 409–13.

Jarratt, S. C. 2014. 'Untimely Historiography? Foucault's "Greco-Latin Trip"', *RSQ* 44: 220–33.

Jaspers, K. 1953. *The Origin and Goal of History*. Translated by M. Bullock. London, Routledge & Kegan Paul. First published in German 1949.

Johnson, D. M. 2005a. 'Persians as Centaurs in Xenophon's *Cyropaedia*', *TAPhA* 135: 177–207.

————. 2005b. 'Xenophon at His Most Socratic (*Memorabilia* 4.2)', *OSAPh* 29: 39–73.

————. 2009. 'Aristippus at the Crossroads: The Politics of Pleasure in Xenophon's *Memorabilia*', *Polis* 26: 204–22.

————. 2021. *Xenophon's Socratic Works*. Abingdon, Routledge.

————. 2024. 'Women in Xenophon's Socratic Works', in S. Brill and C. McKeen (eds.), *The Routledge Handbook of Women and Ancient Greek Philosophy*. New York, Routledge, 135–50.

Johnstone, S. 1994. 'Virtuous Toil, Vicious Work: Xenophon on Aristocratic Style', *CPh* 89: 219–40.

Kallet, L. 2003. '*Demos tyrannos*: Wealth, Power, and Economic Patronage', in Morgan 2003: 117–53.

Keim, B. 2018. 'Xenophon's *Hipparchikos* and the Athenian Embrace of Citizen *Philotimia*', *Polis* 35: 499–522.

Kennedy, R. F. 2014. *Immigrant Women in Athens. Gender, Ethnicity, and Citizenship in the Classical City*. New York, Routledge.

Konijnendijk, R. 2018. *Classical Greek Tactics. A Cultural History*. Leiden, Brill.

Konstan, D. 1997. *Friendship in the Classical World*. Cambridge, Cambridge University Press.

Krentz, P. 1982. *The Thirty at Athens*. Ithaca, NY, Cornell University Press.

L'Allier, L. 2008. 'Une tentative d'explication de la diatribe contre les sophistes: de *L'Art de la chasse* de Xénophon', *CEA* 45: 63–86.

Lachance, G. 2018. 'Xenophon and the Elenchos: A Formal and Comparative Analysis', in Danzig et al. 2018: 165–83.

Laforse, B. 2000. 'Xenophon's Clearchus', *SyllClass* 11: 74–88.

Laks, A. and Most, G. W. 2016. *Early Greek Philosophy. Volume 8, Sophists. Part 1.* Cambridge, MA, Harvard University Press.

Lampe, K. 2015. *The Birth of Hedonism. The Cyrenaic Philosophers and Pleasure as a Way of Life.* Princeton, NJ, Princeton University Press.

Lane, M. S. 2016. 'Popular Sovereignty as Control of Office-Holders: Aristotle on Greek Democracy', in R. Bourke and Q. Skinner (eds.), *Popular Sovereignty in Historical Perspective.* Cambridge, Cambridge University Press: 52–72.

Lane Fox, R. (ed.) 2004. *The Long March. Xenophon and the Ten Thousand.* New Haven, CT, Yale University Press.

Lear, A. 2015. 'Was Pederasty Problematized?', in M. Masterson, N. S. Rabinowitz, and J. Robson (eds.), *Sex in Antiquity. Exploring Gender and Sexuality in the Ancient World.* New York, Routledge: 115–36.

Lee, J. W. I. 2005. 'Xenophon's *Anabasis* and the Origins of Military Autobiography', in A. Vernon (ed.), *Arms and the Self. War, the Military and Autobiographical Writing.* Kent, OH, Kent State University Press: 41–60.

———. 2008. *A Greek Army on the March. Soldiers and Survival in Xenophon's Anabasis.* Cambridge, Cambridge University Press.

Lenfant, D. (ed. and trans.) 2004. *Ctésias de Cnide. La Perse, l'Inde, autres fragments.* Paris, Les Belles Lettres.

Lloyd, G. E. R. 1966. *Polarity and Analogy. Two Types of Argumentation in Early Greek thought.* Cambridge, Cambridge University Press.

Long, A. A. 2005. 'Law and Nature in Greek Thought', in D. Cohen and M. Gagarin (eds.), *The Cambridge Companion to Ancient Greek Law.* Cambridge, Cambridge University Press: 412–30.

Loraux, N. 1982. '*Ponos*: sur quelques difficultés de la peine comme nom du travail', *AION(archeol)* 4: 171–92.

———. 1986. *The Invention of Athens. The Funeral Oration in the Classical City.* Translated by A. Sheridan. Cambridge, MA, Harvard University Press. First published in French 1981.

Low, P. 2018. 'Panhellenism without Imperialism? Athens and the Greeks before and after Chaeronea', *Historia* 67: 454–71.

Luccioni, J. 1948. *Les Idées politiques et sociales de Xénophon.* Paris, Ophrys.

Luraghi, N. 2015. 'Anatomy of the Monster: The Discourse of Tyranny in Ancient Greece', in H. Börm and W. Havener (eds.), *Antimonarchic Discourse in Antiquity.* Stuttgart, Steiner: 67–84.

Machiavelli, N. 1970. *The Discourses*, ed. B. Crick, translated by Leslie J. Walker. Harmondsworth, Penguin. First published in Italian 1531.

————. 1988. *The Prince*. Edited by Q. Skinner and R. Price. Cambridge, Cambridge University Press. First published in Italian 1532.

Marincola, J. 2017. *On Writing History. From Herodotus to Herodian*. London, Penguin.

Mársico, C. 2023. 'How to Become a Successful Tyrant: Ethics and Anthropology in Xenophon's *Hiero*', in C. Mársico and D. R. Nunes Lopes (eds.), *Xenophon, the Philosopher. Argumentation and Ethics*. Berlin, Peter Lang: 149–64.

McClure, L. 2015. 'Courtesans Reconsidered: Women in Aristophanes' *Lysistrata*', *Eugesta* 5: 54–84.

McCoy, M. B. 1999. 'Socrates on Simonides: The Use of Poetry in Socratic and Platonic Rhetoric', *Ph&Rh* 32: 349–67.

McGlew, J. F. 1993. *Tyranny and Political Culture in Ancient Greece*. Ithaca, NY, Cornell University Press.

McNamara, C. 2009. 'Socratic Politics in Xenophon's *Memorabilia*', *Polis* 26: 223–45.

Melville, C. P. and Mitchell, L. G. (eds.) 2013a. *Every Inch a King. Comparative Studies on Kings and Kingship in the Ancient and Medieval Worlds*. Leiden, Brill.

————. 2013b. 'Every Inch a King: Kings and Kingship in the Ancient and Medieval Worlds', in Melville and Mitchell 2013a: 1–20.

Miller, W. (ed.) 1914. *Xenophon. Cyropaedia*. Cambridge, MA, Harvard University Press.

Miltsios, N. 2022. 'Xenophon and Arrian: Aspects of Leadership in Their Anabases', in Rood and Tamiolaki 2022: 329–44.

Missiou, A. 1993. 'Δοῦλος τοῦ βασιλέως: The Politics of Translation', *CQ* 43: 377–91.

Mitchell, L. G. 2023. *Cyrus the Great. A Biography of Kingship*. London, Routledge.

Moore, C. 2013. 'Chaerephon the Socratic', *Phoenix* 67: 284–300.

————. 2015. *Socrates and Self-Knowledge*. Cambridge, Cambridge University Press.

————. 2023. *The Virtue of Agency. Sôphrosunê and Self-Constitution in Classical Greece*. New York, Oxford University Press.

Morgan, K. A. (ed.) 2003. *Popular Tyranny. Sovereignty and Its Discontents in Ancient Greece*. Austin, TX, University of Texas Press.

Morrison, D. R. 1987. 'On Professor Vlastos' Xenophon', *AncPhil* 7: 9–22.

Murnaghan, S. 1988. 'How a Woman Can Be More Like a Man: The Dialogue Between Ischomachus and His Wife in Xenophon's *Oeconomicus*', *Helios* 15: 9–22.

Nadon, C. 1996. 'From Republic to Empire: Political Revolution and the Common Good in Xenophon's *Education of Cyrus*', *American Political Science Review* 90: 361–74.

————. 2001. *Xenophon's Prince. Republic and Empire in the Cyropaedia.* Berkeley, CA, University of California Press.

Nails, D. 2002. *The People of Plato. A Prosopography of Plato and Other Socratics.* Indianapolis, IN, Hackett.

Narcy, M. 1995. 'Le choix d'Aristippe (Xénophon, *Mémorables* II 1)', in G. Giannantoni (ed.), *La tradizione socratica. Seminario di studi.* Naples, Bibliopolis: 71–87.

Natali, C. 1995. '*Oikonomia* in Hellenistic Political Thought', in A. Laks and M. Schofield (eds.), *Justice and Generosity. Studies in Hellenistic Social and Political Philosophy.* Cambridge, Cambridge University Press: 95–128.

Nelsestuen, G. A. 2017. '*Oikonomia* as a Theory of Empire in the Political Thought of Xenophon and Aristotle', *GRBS* 57: 74–104.

Newell, W. R. 1983. 'Tyranny and the Science of Ruling in Xenophon's *Education of Cyrus*', *Journal of Politics* 45: 889–906.

Niebuhr, B. G. 1827. 'Über Xenophons Hellenika', *RhM* 1: 194–8.

North, H. 1966. *Sophrosyne. Self-Knowledge and Self-Restraint in Greek Literature.* Ithaca, NY, Cornell University Press.

Ober, J. 1989. *Mass and Elite in Democratic Athens. Rhetoric, Ideology, and the Power of the People.* Princeton, NJ, Princeton University Press.

————. 2022. *The Greeks and the Rational. The Discovery of Practical Reason.* Oakland, CA, University of California Press.

Ollier, F. 1943. *Le Mirage spartiate. Étude sur l'idéalisation de Sparte dans l'antiquité grecque du début de l'école cynique jusqu'à la fin de la cité.* Paris, Les Belles Lettres.

Osborne, R. 2001. 'The Use of Abuse: Semonides 7', *PCPhS* 47: 47–64.

————. 2003. 'Changing the Discourse', in Morgan 2003: 251–72.

————. 2017. *The Old Oligarch. Pseudo-Xenophon's Constitution of the Athenians.* Third edition. London, London Association of Classical Teachers.

Pangle, T. L. 2018. *The Socratic Way of Life. Xenophon's Memorabilia.* Chicago, IL, University of Chicago Press.

————. 2020. *Socrates Founding Political Philosophy in Xenophon's Economist, Symposium and Apology.* Chicago, Chicago University Press.

Parker, R. 2007. *Polytheism and Society at Athens.* Oxford, Oxford University Press.

Parker, V. 1998. 'Τύραννος: The Semantics of a Political Concept from Archilochus to Aristotle', *Hermes* 126: 145–72.

Pentassuglio, F. 2017. *Eschine di Sfetto. Tutte le testimonianze.* Turnhout, Brepols.

Phillips, A. A. and Willcock, M. M. (ed. and trans.) 1999. *Xenophon and Arrian. On Hunting (Kynēgetikos).* Warminster, Aris & Phillips.

Pomeroy, S. B. 1994. *Xenophon, Oeconomicus. A Social and Historical Commentary.* Oxford, Clarendon.

Pontier, P. 2006. *Trouble et ordre chez Platon et Xénophon.* Paris, Librarie Philosophique J. Vrin.

———. 2018. 'Praising the King's Courage: From the *Evagoras* to the *Agesilaus*', *Trends in Classics* 10: 101–13.

Pownall, F. S. 2000. 'Shifting Viewpoints in Xenophon's *Hellenika*: The Arginusae Episode', *Athenaeum* 88: 499–513.

———. 2004. *Lessons from the Past. The Moral Use of History in Fourth-Century Prose.* Ann Arbor, MI, University of Michigan Press.

———. 2019. 'Violence and Civil Strife in Xenophon's *Hellenica*', in A. Kapellos (ed.), *Xenophon on Violence.* Trends in Classics Supplementary Volumes. Berlin, De Gruyter: 67–82.

Price, A. W. 1997. *Love and Friendship in Plato and Aristotle.* Oxford, Clarendon Press.

Prince, S. H. 2015. *Antisthenes of Athens. Texts, Translations, and Commentary.* Ann Arbor, MI, University of Michigan Press.

Raaflaub, K. A. 2003. 'Stick and Glue: The Function of Tyranny in Fifth-Century Athenian Democracy', in Morgan 2003: 59–93.

Rademaker, A. 2005. *Sophrosyne and the Rhetoric of Self-Restraint. Polysemy and Persuasive Use of an Ancient Greek Value Term.* Leiden, Brill.

Rasmussen, P. J. 2009. *Excellence Unleashed. Machiavelli's Critique of Xenophon and the Moral Foundation of Politics.* Lanham, MD, Lexington.

Reisert, J. 2009. 'Ambition and Corruption in Xenophon's *Education of Cyrus*', *Polis* 26: 296–315.

Rhodes, P. J. 1972. *The Athenian Boule.* Oxford, Clarendon Press.

———. 1993. *A Commentary on the Aristotelian Athenaion Politeia.* Second edition. Oxford, Clarendon Press.

———. 2006. 'The Reforms and Laws of Solon: An Optimistic View', in J. Blok and A. P. M. H. Lardinois (eds.), *Solon of Athens. New Historical and Philological Approaches.* Leiden, Brill: 248–60.

Ricks, T. E. 2020. *First Principles. What America's Founders Learned from the Greeks and Romans and How That Shaped Our Country.* New York, HarperCollins.

Riesbeck, D. J. 2016. *Aristotle on Political Community.* Cambridge, Cambridge University Press.

Rijksbaron, A. 2002. 'The Xenophon Factory: 150 Years of School Editions of Xenophon's *Anabasis*', in R. K. Gibson and C. S. Kraus (eds.), *The Classical Commentary. Histories, Practices, Theory.* Leiden, Brill: 235–67.

Roisman, J. 1989. 'Klearchos in Xenophon's *Anabasis*', *SCI* 8–9: 30–52.

Rood, T. 1998. *Thucydides. Narrative and Explanation*. Oxford, Clarendon Press.

———. 2004a. 'Panhellenism and Self-Presentation: Xenophon's Speeches', in Lane Fox 2004: 305–29.

———. 2004b. *The Sea! The Sea! The Shout of the Ten Thousand in the Modern Imagination*. (London, Duckworth.

———. 2004c. 'Xenophon and Diodorus: Continuing Thucydides', in Tuplin and Azoulay 2004: 341–95.

———. 2005. 'Introduction', in T. Rood (ed.) and R. Waterfield (trans.), *Xenophon. The Expedition of Cyrus*. Oxford, Oxford University Press.

———. 2010. *American Anabasis. Xenophon and the Idea of America from the Mexican War to Iraq*. London, Duckworth.

———. 2012a. 'The Plupast in Xenophon's *Hellenica*', in J. Grethlein and C. B. Krebs (eds.), *Time and Narrative in Ancient Historiography. The 'Plupast' from Herodotus to Appian*. Cambridge, Cambridge University Press: 76–94.

———. 2012b. 'Xenophon', in I. De Jong (ed.), *Space in Ancient Greek Literature*. Leiden, Brill: 161–78.

———. 2015. 'Political Thought in Xenophon: Straussian Readings of the *Anabasis*', *Polis* 32: 143–65.

———. 2017a. 'Xenophon's Changing Fortunes in the Modern World', in Flower 2017: 435–48.

———. 2017b. 'Xenophon's Narrative Style', in Flower 2017: 263–78.

———. and Tamiolaki, M. (eds.) 2022. *Xenophon's Anabasis and Its Reception*. Trends in Classics Supplementary Volumes. Berlin, De Gruyter.

———., Atack, C., and Phillips, T. 2020. *Anachronism and Antiquity*. London, Bloomsbury.

Root, M. C. 1979. *The King and Kingship in Achaemenid Art. Essays on the Creation of an Iconography of Empire*. Leiden, Brill.

———. 2013. 'Defining the Divine in Achaemenid Persian Kingship: The View from Bisitun', in Melville and Mitchell 2013a: 23–65.

Rosenmeyer, P. A. 2001. *Ancient Epistolary Fictions. The Letter in Greek Literature*. Cambridge, Cambridge University Press.

Russell, B. 1945. *A History of Western Philosophy. And Its Connection with Political and Social Circumstances from the Earliest Times to the Present Day*. New York, Simon and Schuster.

Sandridge, N. B. 2012. *Loving Humanity, Learning, and Being Honored. The Foundations of Leadership in Xenophon's Education of Cyrus*. Cambridge, MA, Harvard University Press.

Sansone, D. 2004. 'Heracles at the Y', *JHS* 124: 125–42.

———. 2015. 'Xenophon and Prodicus' Choice of Heracles', *CQ* 65: 371–77.

Schleiermacher, F. 1987. 'Über den Werth des Sokrates als Philosophen', in A. Patzer (ed.), *Der historische Sokrates*. Darmstadt, Wissenschaftliche Buchgesellschaft, 41–58.

Schmitt Pantel, P. 1992. 'The Difference Between the Sexes: History, Anthropology and the Greek City', in M. Perrot (ed.), *Writing Women's History*, trans. F. Pheasant. Oxford, Blackwell: 70–89.

Schofield, M. 1990. 'Ideology and Philosophy in Aristotle's Theory of Slavery', in *Aristoteles' Politik. Akten des XI. Symposium Aristotelicum*. Göttingen, Vandenhoeck & Ruprecht: 1–27.

———. 1998. 'Political Friendship and the Ideology of Reciprocity', in P. Cartledge, P. Millett, and S. von Reden (eds.), *Kosmos. Essays in Order, Conflict and Community in Classical Athens*. Cambridge, Cambridge University Press: 37–51.

———. 2007. 'The Noble Lie', in G. R. F. Ferrari (ed.), *The Cambridge Companion to Plato's Republic*. Cambridge, Cambridge University Press: 138–64.

———. 2021. 'Plato, Xenophon, and the Laws of Lycurgus', *Polis* 38: 450–72.

———. 2023. *How Plato Writes. Perspectives and Problems*. Cambridge, Cambridge University Press.

Schwartz, E. 1889. 'Quellenuntersuchungen zur griechischen Geschichte. II', *RhM* 44: 161–93.

Sebell, D. 2021. *Xenophon's Socratic Education. Reason, Religion, and the Limits of Politics*. Philadelphia, PA, University of Pennsylvania Press.

Sedley, D. N. 2007. *Creationism and Its Critics in Antiquity*. Berkeley, CA, University of California Press.

Shear, J. L. 2011. *Polis and Revolution. Responding to Oligarchy in Classical Athens*. Cambridge, Cambridge University Press.

Stadter, P. A. 1991. 'Fictional Narrative in the *Cyropaideia*', *AJPh* 112: 461–91.

Sterne, L. 1967. *The Life and Opinions of Tristram Shandy, Gentleman*. Edited by G. Petrie and C. Ricks. Harmondsworth, Penguin. First published 1759–67.

Strathern, A. 2019. *Unearthly Powers. Religious and Political Change in World History*. Cambridge, Cambridge University Press.

Strauss, B. S. 1993. *Fathers and Sons in Athens. Ideology and Society in the Era of the Peloponnesian War*. London, Routledge.

Strauss, L. 1959. *What is Political Philosophy? And Other Studies*. Glencoe, IL, Free Press.

———. 1970. *Xenophon's Socratic Discourse. An Interpretation of the Oeconomicus*. Ithaca, NY, Cornell University Press.

———. 1972. *Xenophon's Socrates*. Ithaca, NY, Cornell University Press.

———. 2013. *On Tyranny, Revised and Enlarged*. Expanded edition. Chicago, IL, University of Chicago Press. First published 1968.

Strazdins, E. 2022. '*Anabasis* as Monument: Arrian, Xenophontic Space, and Literary Authority', in Rood and Tamiolaki 2022: 311–28.

Tamiolaki, M. 2016a. 'Athenian Leaders in Xenophon's *Memorabilia*', *Histos Supplement*: 1–49.

——— 2016b. Review of Buzzetti 2014, *CJ* 111: 379–82.

——— 2018. 'Xenophon's Conception of Friendship in *Memorabilia* 2.6 (with Reference to Plato's *Lysis*)', in Danzig et al. 2018: 433–60.

——— 2019. 'Becoming a Leader in the Household: The Wife of Ischomachus as a Model Leader in Xenophon's *Oeconomicus*', *Sage Business Cases. Ancient Leadership*. https://doi.org/10.4135/9781526487247.

——— 2020a. 'Leaders Managing Negative Emotions: The Episode Between Cyrus and Cyaxares in Xenophon's *Cyropaedia*', *Sage Business Cases. Ancient Leadership*. https://doi.org/10.4135/9781529718447.

——— 2020b. 'Straussian Readings of the *Cyropaedia*: Challenges and Controversies', in B. Jacobs (ed.), *Ancient Information on Persia Re-assessed. Xenophon's Cyropaedia. Proceedings of a Conference Held at Marburg in Honour of Christopher J. Tuplin, December 1–2, 2017.* Classica et Orientalia. Wiesbaden, Harrassowitz: 367–87.

Tatum, J. 1989. *Xenophon's Imperial Fiction. On the Education of Cyrus.* Princeton, NJ, Princeton University Press.

Thesleff, H. 1978. 'The Interrelation and Date of the *Symposia* of Plato and Xenophon', *BICS* 25: 157–70.

Too, Y. L. 2021. *Xenophon's Other Voice. Irony as Social Criticism in the 4th Century BCE.* London, Bloomsbury Academic.

Trédé, M. 1992. *Kairos, l'à-propos et l'occasion. (Le mot et la notion, d'Homère à la fin du IVe siècle avant J.-C.).* Paris, Klincksieck.

Tritle, L. A. 2004. 'Xenophon's Portrait of Clearchus: A Study in Post-Traumatic Stress Disorder', in Tuplin and Azoulay 2004: 325–39.

Tsouna, V. 2020. 'Aristippus of Cyrene', in D. Wolfsdorf (ed.), *Early Greek Ethics*. Oxford, Oxford University Press: 380–411.

Tsouna-McKirahan, V. 1994. 'The Socratic Origins of the Cynics and the Cyrenaics', in Vander Waerdt 1994: 367–91.

Tuplin, C. J. 1993. *The Failings of Empire. A Reading of Xenophon Hellenica 2.3.11–7.5.27.* Stuttgart, F. Steiner.

———. 1994. 'Xenophon, Sparta and the *Cyropaedia*', in A. Powell and S. Hodkinson (eds.), *The Shadow of Sparta*. London, Routledge: 127–64.

———. 2010. 'Xenophon and Achaemenid Courts: A Survey of Evidence', in B. Jacobs and R. Rollinger (eds.), *Der Achämenidenhof.* Wiesbaden, Harrassowitz: 189–230.

———. 2013. 'Xenophon's *Cyropaedia*: Fictive History, Political Analysis and Thinking with Iranian Kings', in Melville and Mitchell 2013a: 67–90.

———. 2014. 'Le salut par la parole: les discours dans l'*Anabase* de Xénophon', in P. Pontier (ed.), *Xénophon et la rhétorique*. Paris, Presses de l'Université Paris-Sorbonne: 69–120.

———. and Azoulay, V. (eds.) 2004. *Xenophon and His World. Papers from a Conference Held in Liverpool in July 1999*. Stuttgart, Steiner.

Vander Waerdt, P. A. (ed.) 1994. *The Socratic Movement*. Ithaca, NY, Cornell University Press.

Vidal-Naquet, P. 1968. 'The Black Hunter and the Origin of the Athenian Ephebeia', *PCPhS* 14: 49–64.

Vlassopoulos, K. 2013. *Greeks and Barbarians*. Cambridge, Cambridge University Press.

Vlastos, G. 1957. 'The Paradox of Socrates', *Queen's Quarterly* 64: 496–516.

———. 1991. *Socrates. Ironist and Moral Philosopher*. Ithaca, NY, Cornell University Press.

———. 1994. *Socratic Studies*. Edited by M. Burnyeat. Cambridge, Cambridge University Press.

Warner, R. (trans.) and Cawkwell, G. (ed.) 1972. *Xenophon. The Persian Expedition* Harmondsworth, Penguin.

Whitehead, D. (ed. and trans.) 2019. *Xenophon. Poroi (Revenue-Sources)*. Oxford, Oxford University Press.

Whitmarsh, T. 2018. *Dirty Love. The Genealogy of the Ancient Greek Novel*. New York, Oxford University Press.

Wilding, L. A. 1957. *Greek for Beginners*. London, Faber and Faber.

Wohl, V. 2002. *Love among the Ruins. The Erotics of Democracy in Classical Athens*. Princeton, NJ, Princeton University Press.

———. 2004. 'Dirty Dancing: Xenophon's *Symposium*', in P. Murray and P. Wilson (eds.), *Music and the Muses. The Culture of Mousike in the Classical Athenian City*. Oxford, Oxford University Press: 337–64.

Wolpert, A. 2019. 'Xenophon on the Violence of the Thirty', in A. Kapellos (ed.), *Xenophon on Violence*. Trends in Classics Supplementary Volumes. Berlin, De Gruyter: 169–86.

Zatta, C. 2009. 'Making History Mythical: The Golden Age of Peisistratus', *Arethusa* 43: 21–62.

Zuolo, F. 2017. 'Xenophon's *Hiero*: Hiding Socrates to Reform Tyranny', in A. Stavru and C. Moore (eds.), *Socrates and the Socratic Dialogue*. Leiden, Brill: 564–76.

Index Locorum

General Index